New Light
on the
Gospels

New Light on the Gospels

Clifford A. Wilson

Foreword by
Professor F. F. Bruce

BAKER BOOK HOUSE
Grand Rapids, Michigan

© 1970 by Clifford Wilson
Reprinted 1975 by
Baker Book House
ISBN: 0-8010-9567-0

Cover photo by Dick L. Van Halsema
Grand Rapids

Printed in the United States of America

Foreword

I welcome the opportunity to contribute a few words by way of introduction to Mr. Wilson's chapters on the light thrown by Near Eastern archaeology on the Gospel records. The subject is one to which he has paid special attention, as Director of the Australian Institute of Archaeology, and these chapters are based on a series of radio talks which have been deemed worthy of a wider public.

In reading such a work as this it is good to realise that it is not a question of proving the truth of the Gospel records. For one thing, archaeology cannot prove the central message of the Gospels—that Jesus Christ is the Son of God and Saviour of the world. For another thing, the Gospel narrative needs no 'proving' at this time of day. No comparable group of documents in the world has been subjected to such detailed and analytical scrutiny as the Gospels have received during the past two centuries, and the upshot of this scrutiny is that they are well established as primary sources in their own right—not only for the story of Jesus but also for the other features of first-century life which they touch. The value of such a book as Mr. Wilson's lies in the clarity with which it brings home to us that the Gospels deal with real people, real places, real events. Even today too many readers of the Gospels cannot rid themselves easily of the idea that there is a certain unreality about their contents: that the characters whom they portray walk, as someone has said, with their feet six inches above the ground. The following pages show how perfectly the persons and incidents of the Gospels fit into the place and time to which they belong. It is precisely because they are so matter-of-fact and down-to-earth in their depiction of the ordinary ways of life that the Gospels make the greater impression when they tell how, in a real human life spent amid those ordinary ways, God acted decisively and once for all for the redemption of mankind.

F. F. BRUCE

Contents

Preface

The present volume is the first of the *New Light* series, the companion volume being *New Light on New Testament Letters*. The series has developed from radio talks first presented in a continuing weekly programme, *Word of Truth*, broadcast over the international radio station H.C.J.B. in Quito, Ecuador.

Special acknowledgment is made to the Council and staff of the Australian Institute of Archaeology, of which Institute the author is Director. Particular thanks should be offered to Mrs. Helen Strang, Miss Margaret Martin, and Mr. David Searle, of the Institute's staff, who have given long hours in this project. Their capable assistance is greatly appreciated.

C.A.W.

TO AVIS

Always encouraging, patient, and interested

Introduction

Is it possible, after nearly two thousand years, for new light to be thrown on the Gospels? The answer is 'Yes' —and the discerning reader will find much of interest in these pages. New light from old letters . . . the relevance of the Dead Sea Scrolls as to the Person of Christ . . . supposed 'new sayings' of our Lord—these are some of the matters discussed. Our aim is to present various aspects on which archaeology and other modern research have thrown light, and to use language that people without special training can understand.

We look over the shoulders of men who wrote at the same time as Matthew and Mark, and Luke and John, and Peter and Paul. In papyrus and other pages from the past we find words and expressions which the New Testament writers also used. Our sacred record glows with even more colour as we read long-forgotten stories now recovered, vividly painting in the background of pictures presented to us in the New Testament.

The Stream Continues to Flow!

As to the papyrus letters from Egypt, the criticism could be raised, "Why bother to go over this old material?" and to this there is an answer.

Much was written about these new findings in the early years of this century, but even as late as 1922 the famous palaeographist Sir Frederic Kenyon had this comment as to the relevance of the papyrus documents to the New Testament:

> "The present generation cannot wait until the stream has ceased to flow. Here, as in other fields of knowledge, it is useful from time to time to make provisional surveys of results, and to leave future years to correct and amplify our conclusions in the light of fuller evidence. It is only necessary to warn one's readers that the conclusions here offered are provisional and make no claim to finality."[1]

Even now it is not possible fully to assess the results of the papyrus findings of the last century, and in this book we merely attempt to bring some aspects into focus. The amount of material available is too great to include it all. Over fifty years ago Professor A. S. Hunt wrote that there was a mass of texts to be sifted and digested,[2] and he suggested this process would take years to complete.

He was right; and this volume is a recognition of that continuing need. And while considering the papyri we have brought together much other relevant material which in this generation has thrown "New Light On The Gospels".

REFERENCES

[1] *J.E.A.* VIII (1922), p. 130.
[2] *Ibid.* I (1914), p. 82.

1

Pages From The Past

As long ago as 1863, Bishop Lightfoot declared his belief in the genuineness of New Testament words. He suggested that those words which were then unknown apart from the Scriptures "probably had been part of the common speech all along. I will go further, and say that if we could only recover letters that ordinary people wrote to each other without any thought of being literary, we should have the greatest possible help for the understanding of the language of the New Testament generally."[1]

"If we could only recover letters of ordinary people." It almost seems that the honoured Bishop was prophetic, for those pages from the past *have* been recovered. Thousands of letters which ordinary people wrote to each other are now in famous libraries around the world. Most of them—dating to the centuries before, during and after New Testament times—were written on papyrus, a reed found in Egypt. Some of the documents were inscribed on ostraca—sherds from broken pots, pieces of pottery on which men wrote. Others were written on pieces of wood, bone, metal, stone and even shells.

Papyrus Referred to in the Bible
In John's Second Epistle he says he will not write by means of *paper* and ink, and the word he uses refers to papyrus. The papyrus plant itself is spoken of at

several places in the Scriptures, including Job 8:11, Isaiah 35:7, and Isaiah 38:2.

Moses' ark of bulrushes (Exodus 2:3) was a little boat made of papyrus. There are many examples of papyrus boats being used on the Nile in ancient times, as is shown in tomb inscriptions such as those at Beni Hasen on the Nile. Reed floats used in modern Nubia are still similar.

Thousands of papyrus sheets, potsherds and other 'documents' have cast fresh light on New Testament times. They were not the remains of great libraries, but came from unexpected places such as ancient rubbish heaps where discarded documents from offices, letters from individuals, books of accounts, etc., were thrown —there to wait for nearly two thousand years until their significance was at last understood.

Treasure from a Broken Crocodile
The discovery of the papyrus writings falls into three main periods. In 1778 a Greek papyrus found its way from Egypt to Europe, and in the succeeding one hundred years occasional finds took place, including copies of the poems of Homer.

The second period was shorter, from 1875 to 1895, when large quantities of papyrus were found in the Fayum province of Egypt, dating to the Roman epoch. The names of Drs. A. S. Hunt and B. P. Grenfell are especially linked with this second period, though German, French and Italian investigators also made significant discoveries.

In addition to the findings at ancient Oxyrhynchus —which we shall discuss further—there are other important papyrus collections from Egypt, such as the Tebtunis papyri and the Amherst collection. Hermopolis was another important site.

The third period dated from 1895 and the succeeding years, especially with excavations undertaken in the

Fayum region of middle Egypt by Dr. Grenfell and Dr. Hunt, with Dr. D. G. Hogarth also participating. There is an interesting story as to how one of the most important 'treasure troves' of papyrus was first recognised at its true worth in modern times. It is the story of a disappointing 'dig' that turned into a dramatic discovery.

Dr. Grenfell and Dr. Hunt were excavating towards the end of the last century at Tebtunis in the Fayum region, and their excavations had not been very fruitful.

They had gone to considerable trouble to excavate one particular tomb, but when it was opened they found only mummified crocodiles.

The workmen were ordered to abandon the tomb. In his annoyance at losing the expected 'bucksheesh', one of the men broke the back of a mummified crocodile with a spade. Imagine his surprise when this so-called sacred creature was found to contain great quantities of papyrus—waste paper dating to the centuries immediately before, during, and after New Testament times. Some was as early as the third century B.C.

In ancient Egypt crocodiles were pampered: the writer Herodotus tells us that at Thebes 'sacred' crocodiles were tamed. They had crystal and gold ear-rings put into their ears, and bracelets on their fore-paws. They were treated as well as possible while alive, says Herodotus, and when they died they were embalmed and buried in sacred vaults.[2]

Finding Unrecorded Sayings of Christ
Other important findings soon followed the incident of the crocodile-smashing at Tebtunis. Oxyrhynchus was especially fruitful. This ancient site on the edge of the western desert was one hundred and twenty miles south of Cairo. It was famous in the fourth and fifth centuries A.D. because of the number of churches and monasteries there. Christianity had taken a strong hold,

and the excavators hoped to uncover traces of early Christian activities. Their findings were beyond their wildest dreams. On only the second day of the excavations a small piece of papyrus was found, and a few days later when this was examined personally by Dr. Hunt, he noticed that one of the Greek words was *karphos*—the word for 'mote' in the saying of our Lord about casting out the beam in one's own eye and then seeing clearly to cast out the *mote* from a brother's eye (Matthew 7:5).[3] Dr. Hunt realised this fragment was part of that saying, but in a different form.

The next day Dr. Hunt identified another fragment as part of Matthew 1. Drs. Hunt and Grenfell suggested that possibly they had found part of a library belonging to Christians who died in the persecutions of the early Church. They had come across part of the famous *Logia**—the unrecorded sayings of our Lord, as well as a fragment of the New Testament itself.

The number of fragments found at Oxyrhynchus was enormous, and as a result of these recovered documents we now know that Oxyrhynchus itself was one of the chief towns in Egypt in A.D. 200, even ranking above Memphis.[4] What documents remain hidden in other centres?

It is possible that other sensational discoveries will continue to flow in from ancient Egyptian centres of early Christianity.

Documents Not Mere Invention
One result of the papyrus findings has been the way traditions have been looked at afresh. Dr. Hunt himself wrote that "the first and most important (lesson is) the general confirmation of tradition."[5]

The 'traditions' of the New Testament are not mere

*Discussed further in Chapter 4.

legends. No longer can it be suggested that the New Testament documents were simply inventions. The papyri make it clear that here were people who lived as surely as we of the twentieth century live. Nobody would deny the existence of this Hellenistic culture at Oxyrhynchus during the third century A.D., for, as Drs. Grenfell and Hunt commented, "Invention under these circumstances would be ridiculous."

And the same argument is true of the New Testament documents. The substantial veracity of the New Testament must be accepted in the light of the papyrus findings of the last century.

'Non-literary' Documents

One of the surprising conclusions from the translation of the papyri from Egypt—and also from Syria, Greece and Asia Minor—has been that some New Testament documents are in a sense 'non-literary'. They are not intended by their authors to be preserved as 'literary' documents, such as Plato's 'Republic'. To a great extent they are, humanly speaking, uninhibited. This is well illustrated by several of the letters which Paul wrote: they came from the heart, and were written to meet local circumstances and specific situations of individuals and groups.

The earlier sweeping assessment as to the non-literary nature of *all* the New Testament writings has been modified. For instance, Luke carefully selected his materials from the available sources, both documents and persons, and presented that information systematically (Luke 1:1-3). Something similar can be said about the Epistle to the Hebrews, the First Epistle of Peter, and the Epistle of James. In these writings—and in the Revelation—we move towards 'literature' in the sense that these documents were meant for a wider circulation than would be the case with a private letter. In addition, Dr. Adolf Deissmann's earlier distinction between 'letter' and 'epistle' is not widely accepted to-day.

The Dignity and Beauty of New Testament Language

These New Testament writers were not without their literary contribution, for in their midst was a Paul, and a John, and a Luke, and even a Peter—men aware of the religious, ethical, and cultural problems around them.

The distinctive dignity of the New Testament writings is especially related to 'every-day' people. In ancient literature, Jewish writings were the major exception to the recognised concept of ignoring the 'lower' classes. Theirs was a radically different approach towards ordinary people, and this is reflected in their writings.

And the New Testament documents were an offshoot of those Jewish writings. Thus the 'lower' classes came to life with irresistible vigour, surging on to the pages of history in a new way. The New Testament has given us a living picture of the so-called middle and lower classes, and it is a distinct contrast to the upper classes presented in other ancient writings.

The findings in Egypt and elsewhere, with their great masses of texts written in the *koine* ('common') Greek of the everyday man, made it clear that the New Testament writings were documents of the people, written in *their* language. The Great Teacher whose personality dominates these writings spoke in such a way that "the common people heard Him gladly" (Mark 12:37). He mixed constantly with those 'everyday' people. He even took to Himself the occupation of a carpenter; some of His followers were fishermen; His great Apostle to the Gentiles—though highly educated—was a leather worker, making tents and in other ways working with his hands.

Our New Testament "pages from the past" are an amazingly preserved record of first century Palestine.

The recovered papyri have silenced many an uninformed critic.

Secular "Pages from the Past" Add Their Testimony
The evidence of secular writers has also been clear—from documents that did not need to be excavated nineteen hundred years after they were written. For the New Testament record is not only thoroughly in accord with the background so far as archaeology touches it, but there is also ample testimony from secular writers. Historical records refute arguments challenging the actuality of the Person of Jesus Christ. Roman writers testify to the fact of Christ: not that they wrote to support Christianity, for they violently opposed the new teaching. Because of this their written testimony is even more telling.

Once Christianity was realised to be separate from Judaism, it was resented by Roman authorities, and attempts were made to stamp it out. And as men such as Tacitus and Pliny the Younger* wrote concerning Christians at the time of Nero and Trajan respectively, they referred also to the Founder of this new religion.

The evidence from these and other secular writers is such that there is no case for denying the historical reality of Jesus Christ. And to these secular writers must be added Jewish writers (including Josephus), the early 'Church Fathers' of the centuries immediately following New Testament times, and many papyrus

---

*In Chapter 1 of his book, *What Think Ye Of Christ?*, under the heading "The Witness of Roman Writers to the Beginnings of Christianity", W. J. Beasley, President of the Australian Institute of Archaeology, quotes letters from the Younger Pliny, the Emperor's Reply to Pliny, the Testimony of Tacitus, and extracts from Suetonius in which both Nero and Vespasian refer to the spreading of Christianity. See also J. P. Free's book, *Archaeology and Bible History*, pp. 286–7.

fragments from everyday people, especially in Egypt. In later chapters we examine some of those fragments.

The exact date of the birth of Jesus Christ cannot be fixed with certainty, but the *fact* of His birth and of His ministry in the proximity of the first century A.D. is established beyond possibility of legitimate challenge.

REFERENCES

[1]Milligan, G. *Selections From The Greek Papyri*, p. xx.
[2]Baikie, J. *Egyptian Papyri And Papyrus-Hunting*, p. 287.
[3]*Ibid.*, p. 239, for further discussion.
[4]Grenfell, B. P., and Hunt, A. S. *The Oxyrhynchus Papyri*, Part IV, p. 163.
[5]Hunt, A. S. *J.E.A.* I (1914), p. 86.

2

Archaeology And
The Birth of Christ

What light does the papyrus, and archaeology in
general, throw on the birth of Christ at Bethlehem?
Until comparatively recent times the account of the
enrolment in Luke's Gospel had been challenged, but
now the critical climate has changed. The argument
was that Luke had too many errors of fact to be taken
seriously.

The Enrolment at Bethlehem: Objections Answered
The supposed errors in Luke 2 were:
  (1) That a census (or enrolment) took place in the
      reign of Herod, at the decree of Caesar Augustus;
  (2) That everyone had to return to his ancestral
      home;
  (3) That everyone in the Roman Empire was in-
      volved; and
  (4) That Quirinius was the Governor of Syria.

(1) At the Decree of Caesar Augustus
These criticisms have been answered to some degree,
especially following the archaeological researches of
Professor Sir William Ramsay in the early years of this
century. Subservient kings such as Herod *did* submit
to Augustus and other emperors, and enrolments took
place as suggested by Luke. We even know from

Egyptian records that the enrolments took place at fourteen-yearly intervals, instituted by Caesar Augustus and continuing for over 200 years. We quote from Dr. A. S. Hunt:

> "It is to the papyri that we owe our knowledge of the periodic census ... The object of this census was taxation, and the cycle of fourteen years depended on the fact that fourteen was fixed as the age at which the poll-tax became payable. On the whole subject of taxation the papyri are very full of information ... "[1]

Drs. Grenfell and Hunt have this further comment:

> "The conclusion to which the data from both sides converge is that the fourteen years' census cycle was instituted by Augustus ... Moreover the papyri are quite consistent with St. Luke's statement that this was the 'first enrolment'."[2, 3]

> "Augustus certainly instituted the so-called provincial census or valuation of property throughout the provinces; and there is nothing in the Egyptian papyri inconsistent with the belief that when Augustus instituted the fourteen years' census cycle, he also at the same time ordered a valuation of property, which was the first of a series ... "[4]

This is what Luke said, long before these ancient papyri were recovered. Luke 2:1, 2 date the new census to the time of Augustus, and to the authority of Quirinius in Syria.

(2) and (3) All Returning to the Ancestral Home

Here is an interesting extract from the enrolment dating to A.D. 104:

> "Since the enrolment by households is approaching, it is necessary to command *all* who for any reason are out of their district to return to their own home, in order to perform the usual business of the taxation ... "[5]

Another letter from Egypt is from a man to his

sister, asking her to have him enrolled. "I cannot come," he writes, "See if you can enrol me." Obviously he doubted if his excuse for absence would be acceptable to the authorities, and so he stresses at the end of his letter, "Do not neglect this my sister, and write to me about the enrolment, whether you have done it or not, and reply to me and I will come and enrol myself."[6]

Against this background we are better able to understand what Luke tells us in his Gospel at chapter 2, verses 3, 4: "And all went to be taxed, *every one into his own city*. And Joseph also went up from Galilee, out of the city of Nazareth, into Judaea, unto the city of David, which is called Bethlehem; *because he was of the house and lineage of David*."

Another return is made out by a free woman who declares her own particulars and goes on to write:

> "There is no one else living with me, neither a stranger, nor an Alexandrian citizen, nor a freedman, nor a Roman citizen, nor an Egyptian, in addition to the aforesaid."[7]

Many other census returns make it clear that Romans, Egyptians, freedmen, slaves[8]—'all the world' as Luke puts it—were enrolled. By 'all the world' Luke meant the inhabited world, and archaeology endorses this intention of Caesar Augustus.

The old criticism that Joseph was not obliged to return to his ancestral village of Bethlehem was unfounded. "All must return to their own home," the Edict of A.D. 104 declared, and that is the picture Luke gives as the time approached for the birth of the Son of God at Bethlehem. He was of the House of David, and so Bethlehem was to be the place of birth —just as the prophet Micah had predicted in one of the clearest of the Messianic prophecies of the Old Testament (see Micah 5:2).

(4) "When Quirinius was Governor of Syria"
We referred briefly to the date of our Lord's birth, and

once again archaeology offers a contribution. According to Professor Sir William Ramsay not only was Quirinius Governor of Syria at the time of the census in A.D. 6, but he was also a high official in Central Asia Minor in 8 B.C., in charge of the army, and so he could have been responsible for another census in Syria. Probably the poll tax in Syria was delayed for some time because of a local uprising which it seems that Quirinius was able to repulse.

To support the argument as to Quirinius twice being in authority in Syria, Sir William points to two separate inscriptions. One of these was discovered in Rome, and Sir William himself discovered another in Asia Minor.*

Summarising some of this evidence, Merrill Unger writes: "Ramsay shows that the enrolment of Palestine was delayed until the late summer or fall of 6 B.C."[9] A date of 7 or 6 B.C. would perfectly fit the Biblical record, for we learn that Jesus was born while Herod was King (Matthew 2 : 1ff.), and that Herod ordered the murder of all children two years old and under— thus possibly some time had elapsed since the wise men first visited Herod. He died in 4 B.C. Herod was looking for a young Child rather than a new-born Babe, and this makes it likely that our Lord's birth was about 7 or 6 B.C.—as suggested by Sir William Ramsay.

The fact that we do not date the birth of our Lord at A.D. 1 is not a Biblical error. The date dividing time into B.C. and A.D. was worked out five centuries after the birth of Christ, and certain errors were included in the calculations.

Another possible explanation as to the term 'first census' is that put forward by Drs. Grenfell and Hunt.

*Sir William Ramsay discusses these findings in his fascinating book, *The Bearing Of Recent Discoveries On The Trustworthiness Of The New Testament* (pp. 271ff.). See also *New Testament Times* by Merrill C. Tenney, p. 137.

They said (as we saw earlier), "The papyri are quite consistent with St. Luke's statement that this was the 'first enrolment'." It was the first enrolment in the sense that this was the institution of the poll tax, a system that went on every fourteen years from then until into the third century A.D. They further comment:

> "The presumption therefore seems to us rather in favour of the idea that the orders of Augustus were being carried out in the Roman province of Syria in the later summer and autumn of B.C. 9, or, ... not later than the autumn of B.C. 8."[10]

A further interesting suggestion concerning the 'first census' is mentioned by Nigel Turner.[11] He quotes a Roman Catholic scholar, Lagrange, in saying that the expression 'first census' has a Hellenistic connotation, and instead of meaning 'first' it can mean 'prior to'. Thus, according to Turner, "There is no grammatical reason for not ... supplying the necessary words in the sentence of St. Luke. 'This census was *prior to* (the census) of Quirinius.'"

The Character of Herod
We do not know anything in ancient writings about the slaughter of the infants (Matthew 2), but this fits the character of Herod the Great. In a fit of rage, only five days before his death he had his own son Antipater put to death. The latter had been imprisoned by his father, and when the rumour spread that Herod had died there was wailing in the place and Antipater attempted to bribe a jailor to release him. The rumour was false, and when Antipater's action was reported, the ruthless despot had his son executed.

Herod had no less than ten marriages legalised, and had other sons murdered. Even his wife Mariamne was put to death on Herod's orders, as was her mother Alexandra.

Luke's and Matthew's comments come to life: as in so many other places in their Gospels we are reminded that these statements as to the enrolling and Herod's actions are actual records concerning people who really lived and moved around the countryside of Bible lands.

REFERENCES

[1]Hunt, A. S. *J.E.A.* I (1914), p. 88.
[2]Grenfell, B. P., and Hunt, A. S. *The Oxyrhynchus Papyri.* Part II, p. 211.
[3]See also Milligan, G. *Selections From The Greek Papyri*, p. 44.
[4]Grenfell and Hunt. *The Oxyrhynchus Papyri*. Part II, p. 213.
[5]Papyrus British Museum 904.
[6]Unger, Merrill F. *Archaeology And The New Testament*, p. 64.
[7]Oxy. Pap. No. 255, dating to A.D. 48.
[8]Milligan, G. *Ibid.*, p. 45.
[9]Unger, Merrill F. *Ibid.*, p. 66. See also previous pages for Dr. Unger's discussions on these points.
[10]Grenfell and Hunt. *Ibid.*, p. 212.
[11]Turner, N. *Grammatical Insights Into The New Testament*, pp. 23, 24.

3

Israel's Messiah: The Search . . . The Herald . . . The King!

We shall not discuss the Dead Sea Scrolls in detail, but glance at some aspects relevant to our title "New Light on the Gospels". We are especially interested in the search for the Messiah, then the background of His herald, and with the presentation to His people and to the world of the Messiah Himself.

The manuscripts from the Dead Sea caves were found in 1947 and the following years in three main areas—Qumran, Murabba'at, and at Herod's ancient palace at Masada. Most scholars now accept that the most important scrolls from Qumran dated to the 2nd century B.C.; that those from Masada were hidden before the defeat of the Jewish forces there in A.D. 72; and that the scrolls at Murabba'at were left by the Jewish garrison which participated in the Second Jewish Revolt of A.D. 132.

Our Lord and "The Teacher of Righteousness"

Volumes have been written as to the supposed similarity of the Lord Jesus Christ to the Teacher of Righteousness referred to in the Qumran documents.[1] However, hardly any scholars now seriously suggest that the two were identical, for there were many real differences. This is well illustrated by our Lord's words, "Love your enemies, do good to those who hate you." This opposes the teachings of the Qumran community, as in the scroll known as "The War of the Sons of Light and the Sons of Darkness". The community's enemies were to be destroyed without mercy. Possibly our Lord had this in mind when He said, "You have *heard* that it has been said 'Love your neighbour and hate your enemy', but I say to you 'Love your enemies'."

"The Teacher of Righteousness" was a title, apparently used by successive leaders of the Qumran community. This leader did not display the humility which was typical of Christ. He was deferred to at meals and on other occasions, and his attitude of superiority was very different from the spirit demonstrated at John 13 where our Lord washed His disciples' feet. The Qumran community professed faith in the teachings of their leader, but the disciples of Jesus Christ accepted His teachings and were committed to the Person of their Leader Himself.

Both leaders founded new communities based on Jewish concepts, and their groups were originally limited to Jewish personnel. Both were venerated as God-given leaders. Each presented to his followers a new method of Biblical interpretation, but the incisive thinking and authoritative presentation of Jesus Christ was infinitely superior to the confusion and uncertainty at times associated with the Teacher of Righteousness.

The similarities between the two figures are relatively superficial, and the Teacher of Righteousness never claimed to be the Messiah. On the other hand, Jesus Christ sat by a well in Samaria and told a needy woman, "I am ... the Messiah" (John 4:25, 26). The Teacher of Righteousness looked for a Messiah to come, but Jesus Christ announced Himself as the One sent by the Father.

The Search for the Messiah

The Dead Sea Scroll community was continuing the search that had proceeded over many centuries—a desire growing in intensity through the earlier periods of Jewish History. Old Testament references to the coming Messiah include II Samuel 7:5–16; Amos 9:11–15; Isaiah 9:6, 7; and 11:1ff.; Ezekiel 34:22ff.; Zechariah 3:8; and 6:9ff.; Psalms 2, 72, 89, 110, and 132.

Usually the 'chosen people' associated the idea of prosperity with the advent of the Messiah, though at other times the future hope of prosperity was more important.

Various writings in the Inter-Testamental period as to the Messiah show that the Jewish people were confused.[2] They were groping, comparing Scripture with Scripture, and adding to those Scriptures by their own traditions. There was an air of expectancy, but the problems seemed unanswerable, and some Old Testament statements even seemed contradictory. How could the Messiah be of the line of David and also of the line of Levi—a King who would also be a priest?

Two Messiahs? Or More?

In the Inter-Testamental period this concept developed of two Messiahs—one from Judah, the kingly line, and another from Levi, the priestly line. This, for instance, is the view of "The Testaments of the Twelve Patriarchs", and it is rather similar to what we find with the Dead Sea Scroll community. Thus in the sect's "Manual of Discipline" we read, "... until the coming of a prophet and the Messiahs from Aaron and Israel." As Dr. J. A. Thompson puts it, "The whole society was called 'the community of Israel and Aaron,' and it evidently expected the two Messiahs to emerge from its own ranks."[3]

Sometimes the community speaks of one Deliverer,

at other times of more than one. These figures were to lead the "sons of light" into the expected forty years' war against Belial's army. The Messiah would be "sprinkled with the spirit of truth as purifying water, so as to cleanse him from all abominations of falsehood and from being contaminated with the spirit of impurity."[4]

They expected a Great Prophet, a King, and a Priest of Levi. We may compare the New Testament chapter that tells of Christ being a Priest after another order—the order of Melchisedec—and that He is "holy, harmless, undefiled, separate from sinners" (Hebrews 7:26). He did not need to be "cleansed from all abominations", as with the priestly Messiah expected by the Qumran community!

It is interesting to notice in passing that from another fragment it has become clear that the Dead Sea Scroll community were looking for yet another figure—one after the order of Melchisedec.[5] To the Qumran community Melchisedec appears to have been an angelic being—referring to Isaiah 52:7 they speak of Melchisedec as executing God's judgment against Belial and other evil spirits.

John and the Dead Sea Scrolls Community
Since the findings of the first of the Dead Sea Scrolls in 1947 there has been much speculation as to the possible association of John the Baptist with the Qumran community, near Jericho.[6] Dissatisfied with conditions under the Romans, they left the attractions of the cities to accept the rigours of community life in the wilderness. They established their own monastery, and their "Rules of the Community" were among the Dead Sea Scrolls. Some of their customs had a similarity to the Bible picture of John the Baptist's life. They practised baptism, they lived in the wilderness, they were ascetic in outlook, they quoted Isaiah's prophecy about

"a highway in the desert for our God", and they believed in the soon-coming judgment of God.

But these surface resemblances do not necessarily mean that John was ever actively associated with the Qumran community. They carried out baptism as a daily rite, whereas he gave it a significance far deeper: to him it was not an everyday affair, but a recognition of the need for repentance and a change of life. It was the outward expression of a soul-searching experience—a far more solemn experience than the daily ritual of Qumran.

It is true that John lived for some time in the general area of the Qumran community, for we read at Luke 1:80, "And the child grew, and waxed strong in spirit, and was in the deserts till the day of his shewing unto Israel."

As Professor F. F. Bruce says, "The implication of these words is that, for a number of years preceding the start of his baptismal ministry, John resided in the wilderness of Judaea. Now, if a congenial retreat was found there by a youth who was born in a city of Judaea and was later to be active in the Jordan valley, it would not have been far from the neighbourhood of Qumran. And one who was of priestly birth, as John was, might have found something especially appealing in a movement which attached such importance to the preservation of a pure priesthood."[7]

Then, too, John was ascetic: "And the same John had his raiment of camel's hair, and a leathern girdle about his loins; and his meat was locusts and wild honey" (Matthew 3:4).* The Qumran community were also strict in their way of life—their determination to live out in the wilderness showed that. But they were not dressed as John was, nor did they have such a plain diet. In fact, we know from the excavations that they

*See also Luke 7:33.

ate well. John hardly learned his ideas of a perfect meal (!) from the Dead Sea Scroll community.

A Highway in the Desert

Even the quotation of Isaiah 40:3 as to preparing a highway in the desert for God was interpreted differently by John. The Qumran people saw this verse as a challenge to withdraw into the wilderness. John the Baptist saw it as applying to himself, especially the first part of the verse which speaks of a voice crying in the wilderness. He knew that he himself was that voice, now privileged to proclaim the long-awaited Messiah.

The idea of a 'herald' or 'forerunner' is known outside the Bible. The herald went ahead of the king, clearing his path, and ensuring that all was in readiness for him. John the Baptist was fore-ordained as the herald of the King of Kings. He had the unique distinction of being the only prophet (apart from our Lord) whose own coming was foretold prophetically (Isaiah 40:3 and Malachi 3:1).

History has shown how right John was concerning the Messiah. Tragically, the Jewish people as a nation have continued to reject the one to whom their prophet John the Baptist pointed. They have refused to listen to "the voice crying in the wilderness" and they themselves have continued to know an unsatisfying existence in a spiritual wilderness. They have a form of godliness, but have denied the power thereof (II Timothy 3:5).

The Dead Sea community looked for the coming judgment of God when their wrongs would be righted and their enemies subjugated. John the Baptist also saw that the Kingdom of God was about to be ushered in in a new way, and he pointed to the King Himself, to the one to whom all judgment had been committed.

An Authentic Historical Record

Many aspects of the story of John the Baptist indicate that it is a record of factual history. At Luke 3:1, 2 we read: "Now in the fifteenth year of the reign of Tiberius Caesar, Pontius Pilate being governor of Judaea, and Herod being tetrarch of Galilee, and his brother Philip tetrarch of Ituraea and of the region of Trachonitis, and Lysanias the tetrarch of Abilene, Annas and Caiphas being the high priests, the word of God came unto John the son of Zacharias in the wilderness."

These two verses give a concise statement of historical background, noteworthy for its accuracy in detail. Seven different Roman and Jewish officials are referred to, and we know from other records that Luke was right at every point—instances of the many striking indications of his first-hand knowledge. It is little wonder that Professor Sir William Ramsay considered Luke worthy of a place "among the historians of the first rank."[8]

John the Baptist himself is a thoroughly attested historical person, this being demonstrated from non-Biblical sources. The Jewish historian Josephus, who lived in the first century A.D., wrote at length about him. In his *Antiquities Of The Jews* Josephus referred to Herod's execution of John and to the message he preached; for instance, "... Herod slew him, who was a good man, and commanded the Jews to exercise virtue, both as to righteousness towards one another, and piety towards God, and so to come to baptism ..."[9] Over the centuries the Jewish people themselves have recognised John as a prophet.

"Are You That Prophet?"

At John 1:19, 20 we read of a Jewish deputation coming to John from Jerusalem and asking if he himself claimed to be the Messiah. His answer was 'No,' and then they asked if he was Elijah, the great prophet whom they expected before Christ appeared. When again his answer was 'No,' they asked him, "Are you that Prophet?" John did not ask, "Which Prophet?" for he already knew. He shared his people's hopes as to the Prophet who would come, foretold by Moses at Deuteronomy 18:15–19.

John told the deputation that he was "the voice crying in the wilderness, 'Prepare ye the way of the Lord.'" He pointed on to the Messiah, Jesus of Nazareth, whom he baptised in the River Jordan. John stated clearly that this one was the expected Deliverer, but in the main the Jews rejected his testimony.

Even John did not understand all the Old Testament prophecies, and at one time sent to Jesus asking, "Art Thou He that should come, or should we look for another?" (Matthew 11:3; Luke 7:20).

The early disciples of Christ also did not fully understand, and tended to think of His mission as involving the overthrow of the Roman Empire and the establishment of a new Kingdom, the true Kingdom of God on earth. They had to learn that Christ must first suffer, and that His was primarily a spiritual kingdom.

Summarising, John might have had some contact with the Qumran community, or with another group like them, but his message was radically different from theirs, having a much deeper spiritual challenge. He taught with a new authority: once again, after hundreds of years, the authentic voice of prophecy was heard. As we read at Mark 11:32, "All held that John was a real prophet."

And this historic figure, this authentic prophet, is another reminder of the historical nature of the records about Jesus Christ. "He must increase," said John, "I must decrease." John was right. Having announced the coming of the King, his work was finished and he went to his reward.

A Scroll of Messianic Prophecy

But let us return to the Dead Sea Scroll community at Qumran. Clearly they believed the Messiah or Messiahs would soon appear, and there is evidence from their scroll, that they brought together Old Testament Messianic references. They identified with this Divine Deliverer Scriptures such as Deuteronomy 18:18, 19, specifically referring to the Prophet who would come; Numbers 24 : 15–17, speaking of the expected King; and Deuteronomy 33:8–11, where we read of Moses giving his blessing on the priestly family of Levi. These and other Old Testament Messianic Scriptures were found in one document in Cave 4 at Qumran.

Although they brought these Messianic Scriptures together, they did not associate them with another Old Testament concept clearly relating to the Messiah —that is, the concept of the Suffering Servant in Isaiah, though they did have copies of Isaiah's Prophecy long before Christ was born. These wonderful Servant Songs were interpreted (then and now) by the Jewish people in various ways—as referring to a particular king of Israel, or a great prophet such as Jeremiah, or the nation of Israel, or the faithful remnant who would walk in holiness before their God, or even the individual suffering Jew.

Christ is the Suffering Servant

The New Testament emphasises that the ultimate fulfilment of the Suffering Servant is the Lord Jesus Christ. This is made clear as we watch the evangelist Philip running along the road leading to Gaza, and listening as an Ethiopian eunuch reads one of the Servant Songs aloud. At Acts 8 : 32 we learn that he was reading from Isaiah 53 : 7, 8 : "He was led as a sheep to the slaughter; and like a lamb dumb before his shearer, so opened he not his mouth; in his humiliation his judgment was taken away: and who shall declare his generation? For his life is taken from the earth."

"Do you understand what you are reading?" Philip called out, and the eunuch answered, "How can I, unless someone guides me?" He invited Philip up into the chariot and then asked him, "Tell me, of whom is the prophet speaking? Is he speaking of himself or of someone else?" And we are told (at verse 35), "Then Philip opened his mouth, and began at the same scripture, and preached unto him Jesus." The Suffering Servant was the Lord Jesus Christ, the Messiah of the Jews.

This is also made clear by our Lord Himself at Mark 10:45: "For even the Son of Man came not to be ministered unto, but to minister, and to give His life a ransom for many." In that verse the word 'minister' simply means 'servant'. He did not come to be served but to serve, and His service led to His giving His life a ransom for many. One of the Messianic titles in non-canonical Jewish writings was 'Son of Man'. In this verse (Mark 10:45) the Lord Jesus Christ called Himself 'Son of Man' as well as showing that He was the Suffering Servant.

The Great Prophet

He was the Son of Man—He was the Suffering Servant—and He was the Great Prophet who should come. In the New Testament we read of questions and discussion about Jesus of Nazareth being that Great Prophet. Thus, at John 6:14, after the miraculous feeding of the five thousand, the people declare, "This is of a truth that Prophet who should come into the world." Some of them recognised the similarity to Moses who also had fed his people in the wilderness. Was not this the Christ?

Then again Christ offered spiritual drink at the time of the Feast of Tabernacles, and the people declared,

"This is really the Prophet" (John 7:40). The Feast of Tabernacles was when they remembered they were pilgrims and strangers, looking for the city whose Builder and Maker was God. In the wilderness Moses had struck a rock and water had flowed forth. Now Jesus declared that all who were thirsty could come to *Him* and drink. So the people remembered, and thought in terms of Christ as the fulfilment of the prophecy of Moses.

The same truth is shown at Acts 3:22, where Peter explicitly states that these words of Moses referred to Jesus, and so also does Stephen at Acts 7:37. Stephen's insistence that Jesus was the Christ, the Great Prophet who should come, was a major reason for his violent death.

To summarise, for the first time in Jewish history the seemingly divergent Messianic strands came together beautifully as our Lord applied them to His own Person. He is the Messiah whom God anointed with the Holy Spirit and with power: He is the Son of Man, the one made in the likeness of men; He is the Suffering Servant, the one obedient unto death; He is the great High Priest, not after the constantly changing order of Levi but after the eternal order of Melchisedec; He is the Lamb of God, for this great High Priest offered *Himself* without spot to God. He is the rightful King of the Jews. He is the Prophet like unto Moses, and yet a Greater than Moses, for Moses, like John the Baptist, was but a voice. Jesus Christ spoke with an authority that none could gainsay, for He was Himself the *Logos*, the Word of God.

REFERENCES

[1]Blaiklock, E. M. *Buried History* 3 (Dec. 1967), pp. 5, 6.
[2]*Buried History* 4 (Sept. 1968), pp. 77–80. See also Mann, C. S. *Christianity Today* XII (June 1968), p. 18; and, *Buried History* 3 (June 1967), pp. 7, 8.

[3]Thompson, J. A. *The Bible and Archaeology*, pp. 262, 263.
[4]*Buried History* 4 (Sept. 1968), p. 79.
[5]*Ibid.*, 3 (June 1967), pp. 5–8.
[6]Bruce, F. F. *Second Thoughts on the Dead Sea Scrolls*, pp. 141–144.
[7]*Ibid.*, p. 142.
[8]Ramsay, Sir William. *St. Paul the Traveller and the Roman Citizen*, p. 4.
[9]Whiston, W. (translator). *The Life and Works of Flavius Josephus*, p. 540.

4

The "New Sayings" Of Our Lord

In this century new findings of tremendous interest for the Bible student have come to light. These have included additional sayings supposed to have come from the Lord Jesus Christ. At first sight it is not easy to decide what really came from Him, and where the sayings were added to according to the memories of those who had heard Him. By the time they were committed to writing it was no longer possible to distinguish the original saying from what had been added, and the 'new sayings' simply are not acceptable as are the Canonical Gospels.

One major disappointment is that these early writings include gnostic ideas. Consequently we must be careful in approaching them because they include heretical teaching.

A Comment on the Word 'Gnostic'
Because of this distortion of our Lord's teaching, it is desirable to comment briefly on the word 'gnostic'. It literally means "one who has knowledge", and it came to include the idea that salvation is attained by knowledge of God. Eventually the body and soul are separated because the physical has evil associations and must therefore be entirely sublimated. According to gnosticism, God is unknown, and He did not create this

imperfect world. It is purely a mischance whereby physical man finds himself in such an imperfect state. Escape from the powers of the world is by meditation and rejection of the physical, because matter is evil. Through knowledge of himself, man is able to find release, and to be no longer bound by the tyranny of evil. Thus he can be embraced back into the bosom of God the Absolute.

Gnosticism is a kind of syncretism—an adapting of one culture, including religious beliefs, into one's own system. An early form of gnosticism was strenuously opposed by the Apostle Paul in the Epistle to the Colossians, and by John in his letters at the end of the first Christian century. They were not slow to raise their voices against this evil.

Paul stresses that Jesus Christ created all things—"by Him were all things created" (Colossians 1:16). He further states, "In Him dwells all the fulness of the Godhead bodily" (Colossians 2:9). Christians are complete in Christ (Colossians 2:10). In Christ are hidden all the treasures of wisdom and knowledge (Colossians 2:3). Believing that matter was evil, the gnostics taught that God could not be reached by direct contact with matter. Thus they argued that a series of angelic mediations were necessary for man and God eventually to be brought together. 'No,' said the Apostle Paul, "In Him" —in the Man Christ Jesus—"In Him all the fulness of the Godhead dwelt *bodily*."

Little Emphasis on the Works of Christ

It is now recognised that many of the early 'new sayings' and 'new gospels' were 'gnostic' in their approach. They are to a great extent collections of supposed *sayings* of the Lord Jesus Christ, with little emphasis on His *works*. Some of the sayings are similar, and at times even identical, to those in the synoptic Gospels, but on this matter of the works of Jesus Christ there is a very great difference. This is understandable, for many of these recovered documents came from gnostic sects.

In John's Gospel we read of a whole series of 'signs' —miraculous activities whereby the Lord Jesus Christ demonstrated that He was, and is, God. He who was perfect Man was also God in the fullest sense, and in all the Gospels—synoptics and John alike—His works as well as His words were stressed. Our Lord could say that His doctrine was the Father's—"My doctrine is not Mine, but His that sent Me" (John 7:16), but He could also say that His *works* proved He came from the Father (John 14:10, 11).

New Testament Indications that Others Wrote His Words
We shall look briefly at some of these 'new sayings',[1] and we do not disparage all those which do not appear in the Gospels. The Apostle Paul quoted an otherwise unknown saying of the Lord, "It is more blessed to give than to receive" (Acts 20:35). This is not known in the Gospels, and it gives us a clue that no doubt there were many collections of His words. The incident in John 8 of the woman taken in adultery is not in the earliest manuscripts, but is widely accepted as genuine. It is known in these ancient documents from Egypt.

These two pointers suggest the genuineness of much that is written but is not included in our Gospels. Then again, at the very end of the Gospels, we read, "And there are also many other things which Jesus did, the which, if they should be written every one, I suppose that even the world itself could not contain the books that should be written" (John 21:25). John was using typical eastern language, and he is referring especially to the works of our Lord, but these references taken together make it clear that others besides those privileged to pen the Canonical Gospels wrote of the life and sayings of the Lord Jesus Christ.

As Luke tells us at the beginning of his Gospel, many undertook to "set forth in order a declaration of those things which are most surely believed among us" (Luke 1:1), and probably extracts from some of those collections would have been included in these documents found in Egypt.

As we read these sayings, sometimes there is a sense of reverence as we recognise the possibility that our Lord did say some of the words recorded, for they are consistent with utterances within the Canonical Gospels. In this category are the 'new sayings' which Drs. Grenfell and Hunt published in 1897. These sayings came from Oxyrhynchus, and the paleographic evidence would suggest a date for them of about 200 A.D.[2] The fragment measured about 6 inches by 4 inches.

Casting Out the Mote
The first *logion*—or 'saying'—is perhaps the best accepted, simply because of its similarity to Luke 6:42— "And then thou shalt see clearly to cast out the mote that is in thy brother's eye."

But as we go on through the 'new sayings' we notice changes from the Lord's teaching. Saying No. 2 is: "Jesus saith, Except ye fast to the world, ye shall in no wise find the kingdom of God; and except ye keep the sabbath, ye shall not see the Father." Here are words about finding the Kingdom of God (compare the Kingdom parables of Matthew 13), but then we observe that nowhere in the Canonical Gospels did our Lord enjoin the ritualistic keeping of the Sabbath. He required the keeping of nine commandments, that concerning the Sabbath being the only one He did not specifically prescribe. In fact, by Jewish standards, He Himself broke the Sabbath (John 5:18).

We have a similar sense of caution towards Saying No. 3—"Jesus saith, I stood in the midst of the world, and in the flesh was I seen of them, and I found all men drunken, and none found I athirst among them, and My Soul grieveth over the sons of men, because they are blind in their heart . . ."

This is rather similar to what John gives us in his Prologue—"He came unto His own and His own received Him not." Similar also is His rebuke to the Jews who were spiritually blind. Yet would our Lord say "I found *all* men drunken, and *none* found I athirst among them"? Rather, He found the few athirst, and His teaching to His disciples was that though the way was narrow, there were a few who found it. Instead of saying that He found none *athirst* among men, He would say, "Blessed are they that hunger and thirst after righteousness, for they shall be filled" (Matthew 5:6).

"Cleave the Wood and There Am I"
Sayings Nos. 4 and 8 were almost indiscernible. Probably the best known of the eight sayings is the fifth : "Jesus saith, Wherever there are . . . and there is one . . . alone, I am with him. Raise the stone and there thou shalt find Me, cleave the wood and there am I." This has affinity with Matthew 18:20—where two or three are gathered together in the Lord's Name, He Himself is in the midst. Other scholars suggest that the teaching is that if a righteous person is alone, spiritually he is not alone because the Lord is with him. Others see some similarity to Ephasians 4:6: "There is one God and Father of all, Who is above all, and through all, and in you all."

Saying No. 6 is, "Jesus saith, A prophet is not acceptable in his own country, neither doth a physician work cures upon them that know him." There is a similar statement at Luke 4:24 which also tells us that a prophet is not acceptable in his own country; Matthew 13:57 and Mark 6:4 are also relevant.

The second part of the paragraph has affinity with Luke 4:23—immediately before the statement of a prophet not being accepted in his own country, at verse 23 we read the proverb, "Physician, heal thyself".

The seventh saying is, "Jesus saith, A city built upon the top of a high hill, and stablished, can neither fall nor be hid," and we are reminded both of Matthew 5:14—"A city set on a hill cannot be hid"—and of the reference in Matthew 7 to the house built upon a rock.

Seventeen Sayings About Four Incidents

Another important publication of 'new gospel sayings' was *Fragments of an Unknown Gospel and other Early Christian Papyri*, edited by H. Idris Bell and T. C. Skeat, and issued in 1935. This discussed seventeen newly recovered sayings attributed to Jesus, also believed to be dated to the middle of the second century A.D., and probably coming from Oxyrhynchus—though this was not absolutely established. Scholars suggested that the sayings themselves were compiled before the end of the first century A.D. These sayings of less than one hundred lines caused a great sensation when they were first published. They were quite a different series from those discussed in our last section.

They relate to four episodes—one being a dispute with the rulers of the Jews, which has similarities to John 5:39 as to the accusation of Moses, and to John 9:29 which relates to God speaking with Moses.

The second episode concerns the healing of a leper, and we quote it in full:

"And behold, there cometh unto Him a leper and saith, Master Jesus, journeying with lepers and eating with them in the inn I myself also became a leper. If therefore thou wilt, I am made clean. The Lord then said unto him, I will; be thou made clean. And straightway the leprosy departed from him. And the Lord said unto him, Go and shew thyself unto the priests ..."

The similarity to the story in Matthew 8 is evident. Is this the man's story to the Lord about his leprosy?

The third episode has obvious analogy to the question of the Herodians paying tribute to Caesar, and the fourth is a supposed miracle where new life was apparently given in the general area of the Jordan. Jesus sprinkled something on the Jordan, and fruit was said to appear. Some scholars suggest it might be a practical illustration of the saying, "Except a corn of wheat fall into the ground and die it abideth alone." But the meaning is obscure.

These, and the rest of the seventeen sayings, are interesting and at first sight it appeared they might have been part of another Gospel. However, later findings have shown that virtually all of them were included in gnostic writings, especially in the so-called "Gospel According to Thomas".*

A Supposed Incident in the Temple
Oxyrhynchus Papyrus No. 840 also appears to be a fragment from a lost Gospel, and it tells of a dramatic meeting with a Pharisee in the Temple of Jerusalem. The papyrus is dated to the fourth century, though it is a copy, and the original would have been much older.

We quote as follows:

"And He took them and brought them into the place of purification itself, and He was walking about in the Temple. And a certain Pharisee, a high priest, Levi by name, approached and met them, and said to the Saviour: 'Who permitted Thee to walk this place of purification and to see these holy vessels, when Thou hast not washed

*Discussed in Chapter 5.

45

Thyself, nor yet have Thy disciples bathed their feet? But, being defiled, Thou hast walked this Temple, though it is a clean place, which none other, save one that hath washed himself and changed his garments, walketh, neither dareth he to see these holy vessels.' And straightway the Saviour stood with His disciples and answered him: 'Art thou, being here in the Temple, clean?' The other saith to Him: 'I am clean. For I have washed myself in the pool of David, and by the one stair I descended and by the other I ascended; and I arrayed myself in white garments and clean; and then I came and looked upon these holy vessels.' The Saviour answered and said unto him: 'Woe, ye blind that see not! Thou hast washed thyself with these pouring waters in which dogs and swine have been cast night and day, and hast loved and wiped the outside skin which the harlots and the flute-girls anoint and wash and beautify to excite the lust of men; but within they are filled with scorpions and every sort of wickedness. But I and My disciples, who, thou sayest, have not been bathed, have been bathed in the waters of eternal life that come from (the throne of God)'."

At first sight this appears to be a delightful addition to our knowledge of the Lord Jesus Christ, but closer examination shows it must have been written much later than the times of Christ, probably being compiled in Egypt when the destruction of the Temple was but a vague memory. The document contains obvious indications that it was not genuine.

Our Lord here is called 'the Saviour'. Although the New Testament refers to him as the Saviour in such places as Luke 2:11, John 4:42, Acts 13:23 etc., this is a description of His work rather than a title. The term 'the Saviour' was not used consistently of Christ until post-apostolic times. The incident itself might have been genuine, but the account of it has been embellished with the passage of time. There was no "place of purification" within the precincts of the

Temple, such as is referred to, as though it were a court open to the public. Nor was it required of ordinary worshippers to carry out ablutions, as this fragment would suggest. Neither was there a "Pool of David" approached by one set of stairs and left by another—and certainly there is no record of such a Pool of David being polluted by dogs and swine. Even the reference to "a certain Pharisee" being a high priest is open to suspicion, for the high priests were usually, though not always, Sadducees.

Probably the man who penned this story had heard of it and then put it down in writing, colouring it by his own imagination. The description he gives would suit an Egyptian ritual, and he even includes the expression "harlots and flute girls"—these would be well-known at an Egyptian temple, but certainly not in the Temple at Jerusalem. Even the ideas as to ceremonial ablutions are more Egyptian than Jewish.[3] Most scholars today regard this as a purely apocryphal Gospel portion.

The Superiority of the True Gospels

These ancient writings from Oxyrhynchus and other parts of Egypt are not in the same category as the Canonical Gospels. Over and over again the Canonical Gospels have been investigated, and their local colouring has been found to be accurate. The "Fragments of an Unknown Gospel" quoted above, and the so-called "Sayings of our Lord" which include so much gnostic heresy, helpt to vindicate the authenticity of the Canonical Gospels. These true Gospels are not figments of the imagination, nor even genuine sayings elaborated and added to by the fanciful ideas of men. Rather, these are Scriptures which record the life of the Lord Jesus Christ, as the Holy Spirit Himself brought to men's minds those things whereby Christ would be glorified (John 14:26; 16:13, 14).

REFERENCES

[1] Grenfell, B. P., and Hunt, A. S. *Sayings of Our Lord.* 1897.
[2] *Ibid.*, p. 6.
[3] Discussed further: Smith, D. *Unwritten Sayings of Our Lord*, p. 133.

5

The "New Gospels" And False Teaching

One of the other important sites from which so-called 'gospels' have been recovered is Nag Hammadi, about seventy miles north of Luxor in Egypt. In 1945 local workers found an urn while digging at an ancient church in the area, and when it was opened a great number of manuscripts fell out. Eventually they arrived in three bundles in Cairo, and were offered for sale in 1948. In the succeeding five years they were bought by reputable institutions, and soon the conclusions of scholars were available to the world.

Some of the 'Gospels' and Other Writings Listed
Included among the findings were "The Gospel of the Egyptians", "The Wisdom of Jesus", "The Gospel of Truth", "The Gospel of Thomas", "The Gospel of Philip", "The Book of Thomas, being the sacred words spoken by Jesus to Thomas", "The Acts of Peter", "The Revelation of Paul", "The Revelation of James"—and many others. The texts appear to date from the second half of the *fourth* century, and again they are basically gnostic in outlook.

These heretical groups endorsing gnostic teachings were especially prevalent in Egypt in the fourth century A.D.[1], but they were known there earlier. It is interesting to read that Apollos had been instructed in the Word in his own country (Acts 18:25). As he came from Alexandria, he could have heard Christian teachings in Egypt, but Aquila and Priscilla had to instruct him in the deeper truths of Christianity (Acts 18:26). Was it only on the matter of baptism, or were there other problems as well? Perhaps the early gnosticism which Paul and John refuted was known also to Apollos.

"The Gospel of Thomas"

One of the gnostic writings we have mentioned is "The Gospel of Thomas". More than one "Gospel of Thomas" is referred to in ancient writings. We have already seen that the second collection—the "Fragments of an Unknown Gospel"—are included in almost the same form in this gnostic "Gospel of Thomas".

The preamble is as follows:

> "These are the secret words which the Living Jesus spoke and Didymus Judas Thomas wrote.
> "And He said: Whosoever finds the explanation of these words will not taste death."[2]

So this is a secret revelation, and this is typical of the gnostic approach to wisdom. Thus in a sense these so-called 'gospels' are in opposition to the Canonical Gospels.

These words are supposed to be recorded by Didymus Judas Thomas, but in fact the word 'Didymus' simply means 'twin', as also does 'Thomas'. W. C. van Unnik points out: "In John 11:16, 20:24, and 21:2, the expression 'called Didymus' is appended to this name: this Greek term for a 'twin' is a rendering of the Aramaic 'Thomas', which has the same meaning. The author, however, did not know about the linguistic connection and took both terms to be personal names."[3]

This "Gospel of Thomas" is not an historical survey

of the life of Christ, for these supposed "Sayings of Christ" are similar from beginning to end, with no crisis such as the resurrection of Christ. Again we are impressed that the emphasis is rather on the sayings than on the works of our Lord. These works vindicated the claims of His words in the accepted Gospels, but they are strikingly absent in this gnostic writing. The Lord Jesus Christ is not seen as the Messiah so much as the one who points to the way by which the *knowledge* of God can be gained.

Many of these sayings are opposed to the teachings of Jesus Christ and so must be rejected. Typical of these would be that concerning Mary (probably Mary Magdalene)—the very last saying, No. 114: "Jesus said, See, I shall lead her, so that I will make her male, that she too may become a living spirit, resembling you males. For every woman who makes herself male will enter the Kingdom of Heaven."[4]

The New Testament teaching is that the Christian—man or woman—is one born of the Spirit of God, and we also learn that Scripture is given to us by men who were inspired by the Holy Spirit. Scripture also uses the expression "The witness of the Spirit" (I John 5:6), and as we read these gnostic gospels and come to passages such as this about Mary Magdalene, there is a witness of the Spirit of God to reject them.

Why were such sayings put in the mouth of the Lord Jesus Christ—sayings which at times contradict those recorded in the Canonical Gospels? Perhaps the simplest answer is that pseudepigraphical writing was common in the centuries before and after the days of the New Testament. This writing in the name of another was not regarded as fraudulent, but was accepted as a literary method. Words were put into the mouth of a bygone hero, partly to give a document greater acceptability. This practice was also followed by some heretical writers, and so we find eccentric sayings supposedly uttered by Jesus Christ; and such sayings simply must be rejected.

"The Gospel of Truth"

Similar criticisms can be levelled against the so-called "Gospel of Truth", which again is a book with an obvious gnostic approach. No mention of the word 'sin' occurs in this book, but rather ignorance of God is the great problem. This is merely a caricature of the true Christian revelation. For instance, it has a remarkable explanation concerning the parable of the lost sheep—the one sheep that is lost is not erring man, but God Himself! Again the basic approach of this book is opposed to the concept of redemption in Christ Jesus.

"The Apocryphon of John" and "The Apocryphon of James"

"The Apocryphon of John" apparently originated in circles outside Christianity, and it used materials dated later than the Christian era. It rejects part of the Biblical story of creation and tells us man is in three layers—spiritual, psychic, and material. Salvation depends on man understanding his true position as regards each of these three aspects. This is a philosophical attempt to show how man is equated with God, and it rather reminds us of the searchings of the Greeks four hundred years before Christ, though the philosophy is blended with Biblical terminology and characters.

Yet another of these documents is "The Apocryphon of James", but it is rather different from the clearcut gnosticism of the others at which we have glanced. It recognises that Jesus the crucified is also the risen Lord. This treatise is to do with man's need to make the heavenward journey, made possible because of the descent of Jesus Christ to this world.

James and Peter are supposed to say after the ascension, "We knelt, I and Peter; we gave thanks, we lifted up our hearts on high to heaven; we heard with our ears and saw with our eyes the tumult of wars and sound of a trumpet and a great confusion; and when we ascended out of that place, we lifted up our minds yet higher still; and we saw with our eyes and we heard with our ears the angels' hymns and cries of praise; and angels rejoiced and the lofty ones of heaven sang; and we rejoiced in our turn. After these things our spirits yearned to raise us aloft to the very Majesty of God; and when we were gone up, it was not suffered us to see and to hear anything."[5]

This is a typical Jewish Apocryphal writing, and cannot be accepted with the same assurance that the Christian has towards the orthodox Gospels.

These gnostic and heretical documents fall far short of the teachings of the Gospels. The great command to "go and make disciples of all nations" (Matthew 28 : 19, 20) is lacking in these documents of gnostic teachers who regarded themselves as the privileged finders of wisdom.

"The Gospel of Philip"

Another of these documents is "The Gospel of Philip". This recovered Coptic manuscript is dated by scholars to about A.D. 400, but it seems likely that the original document—probably in Greek—should be dated to the second century A.D. As with "The Gospel of Thomas", there are various statements which do not ring true to the Christian. Thus we read: "A Gentile man does not die, for he has never lived that he should die";[6] and, "Nor again wilt thou be able to see in light without water or mirror. Because of this it is fitting to baptise in the two, in light and water".[7] Or again—"Adam came into being from two virgins, from the Spirit and from the virgin earth. Because of this Christ was born of a virgin, in order that He might set in order the stumbling which came to pass in the beginning".[8] Or as to the fall of man: "There are two trees in paradise. The one produces beasts; the other produces man. Adam ate from the tree which produced beasts, and becoming a beast he begat beasts."[9] We also read: "Men make gods and they worship their creations. It would be fitting for the gods to worship men."[10]

Clear gnostic teaching is shown by 'sayings' such as: "The Logos said: If you know the truth the truth will make you free. Ignorance is a slave, knowledge is freedom. When we recognise the truth we shall find the fruits of the truth in our hearts. If we unite with it, we will bring our fulfilment."[11] Again we are reminded that the essence of the Canonical Gospels is the redemption that is available through Jesus Christ who lived and then died to give us that redemption.

We also read in this "Gospel of Philip": "The Lord went into the dye-works of Levi. He took seventy-two colours and threw them into the vat. He took them out all white."[12] This borders on the magical rather than the miraculous.

"Infancy Gospels"

There are various other so-called 'gospels' which have magical incidents such as these, including 'Infancy Gospels'. We read of a child who is supposed to have run against Jesus and fallen down dead.[13] We read of a man who had been changed into a mule being turned back into a man when Jesus was placed on his back.[14] We are told of Jesus making figures of animals and birds of clay, and then making them walk, fly and take food[15]—and there are many other episodes. These demonstrate how fantasy took over from fact in many of the non-canonical 'gospels' written in the centuries immediately following our Lord's life on earth.

There are also many modern hoaxes foisted on to

the world—to mention a few, "The Unknown Life of Jesus Christ", "The Crucifixion of Jesus, by an Eye-Witness", "The Confession of Pontius Pilate", "The Description of Christ", and "The Death Warrant of Jesus Christ".[16]

Nevertheless, it is also true that genuine sayings of the Lord Jesus Christ might be embedded in "The Gospel of Philip". Here is one choice saying: "When the pearl is cast down in the mud it does not become dishonoured the more, nor if it is anointed with balsam oil will it become more precious. But it has its worth in the eyes of its owner at all times. So with the sons of God wherever they may be. For they have the value in the eyes of their Father."[17]

But our lasting impression is one of caution and even of rejection of much of this 'new' material. How can we accept such sayings as the following? "Philip the Apostle said, 'Joseph the carpenter planted a garden because he needed the wood for his trade. It was he who made the Cross from the trees which he planted. And his seed hung on that which he planted. His seed was Jesus, but the planting was the Cross".[18]

Wise Words Written Before Recent Findings
Dean Farrar wrote as long ago as 1884:

> "The Four Gospels superseded all others and won their way into universal acceptance by their intrinsic value and authority. After 'so many salutary losses'* we still possess a rich collection of Apocryphal Gospels, and, if they serve no other good purpose, they have this value, that they prove for us undoubtedly the unique and transcendent superiority of the sacred records. These bear the

*"Multi conati sunt scribere Evangelia, sed non omnes recepti" ("There are many who have tried to write gospels, but not all have been accepted"), Origen wrote at the beginning of the 3rd century. This quotation indicates his knowledge of spurious 'gospels' of that time.

stamp of absolute truthfulness, all the more decisively when placed in contrast with writings which show signs of wilful falsity. We escape from their 'lying magic' to find support and help in the genuine Gospels. 'And here we take refuge with the greater confidence because the ruins which lie around the ancient archives of the Church look like a guarantee of the enduring strength and greatness of those archives themselves'."[19]

This comment, written nearly a century ago, is just as true today. No other "gospel writing" bears within itself the "intrinsic value and authority" of the Canonical Gospels.

REFERENCES

[1]van Unnik, W. C. *Newly Discovered Gnostic Writings*, p. 18.

[2]*The Gospel According To Thomas*, duplicated copy of English translation in the Library of the Australian Institute of Archaeology.

[3]van Unnik, W. C. *Ibid.*, p. 49.

[4]*The Gospel According To Thomas*.

[5]van Unnik, W. C. *Ibid.*, p. 86 (quotation from translation of the Apocryphon by Puech, H. C., and Quispel, G.).

[6-12]Wilson, R. McL. *The Gospel Of Philip*.

[13-15]James, M. R. *The Apocryphal New Testament*, pp. 81, 82.

[16]Goodspeed, E. J. *Famous 'Biblical' Hoaxes*.

[17,18]Wilson, R. McL. *Ibid.*

[19]Farrar, F. W. *The Messages of the Books*, p. 27.

6

The "Old Gospels"—
Tested And Found True

"My doctrine is not Mine, but His that sent Me," said the Lord Jesus Christ (John 7:16).

Unlike the "new gospels," the old ones have about them what Canon Phillips has referred to as "the ring of truth". In this chapter we shall discuss the Gospels in general. Then in succeeding chapters, we shall select illustrations from the papyri as they are relevant to the records of Matthew, Mark, Luke, and John.

We referred to the finding of thousands of papyrus documents by Drs. Grenfell and Hunt in the Fayum region of Egypt.* They did not immediately recognise the significance of their discovery, but their findings were soon being studied by others. It was especially the great German scholar, Dr. Adolf Deissmann,† who recognised that these documents were in a form of Greek very similar to that employed in the New Testament.

In earlier years there had been considerable learned discussion as regards the language of the New Testament writings, for they varied greatly in style and even vocabulary from the extant classical Greek writings. Scholars talked rather strangely about the New Testament being written in a unique "language of the Holy

*See Chapter 1.
†See Chapter 9.

Spirit", but now Dr. Deissmann pointed out that in fact the New Testament was written in the language of the everyday people of New Testament times. It was *koine* ('common') Greek, the spoken language of the times. This *koine* Greek was a flexible, energetic and graceful language, and was a telling instrument for the apostles and evangelists

Adolf Deissmann was not the first scholar in modern times to suggest that the New Testament language was that of the "man in the street", for in *The Messages of the Books*, published in 1884, Dean Farrar wrote: "In the papyrus rolls of the British Museum (edited for the trustees by J. Forshall in 1839) there are forms and phrases which constantly remind us of St. Paul" (p. 151).

However, Dean Farrar left the matter there and Dr. Deissmann must be credited with the eventual recognition of the use of everyday language in New Testament writings.

Very Few Greek Words Only 'Biblical'

Before the times of Dr. Deissmann's epoch-making exposition, it was commonly suggested that many New Testament words were unknown outside that collection of Books. The list given by Dr. Deissmann, culled from J. H. Thayer's New Testament Dictionary, includes 767 words which were supposedly limited to the New Testament. Dr. Deissmann pointed out that the list was unacceptable even against the knowledge of his times—he demonstrated that Thayer himself recognised a number of these words as occurring in other writings dating to times later than the New Testament. Dr. Deissmann's point was that this does not make them New Testament words, for, as he says, it is improbable that men such as Plutarch borrowed words from the Bible. Clearly Plutarch and the New Testament writers drew from the same common background—the spoken language of the times.

Thus Thayer's list is cut down to about 550 words, but Dr. Deissmann brings the list further down and states:

"I estimate that in the whole New Testament vocabulary of nearly 5,000 words not many more than 50—fewer than that, more likely—will prove to be 'Christian' or 'Biblical' Greek words. I therefore estimate the total of Biblical words in the New Testament as (at the utmost) 1 per cent of the whole vocabulary."[1]

Why Greek?

The question might be asked, "Why is it that the New Testament has been preserved in the Greek language, and why were so many of the New Testament fragments written in Greek?" Actually fragments have been found in various other languages, but Greek was an international language, and if the gospel had been retained in Hebrew or Aramaic it is conceivable that the gospel itself would have been confined to Palestine. To become a religion of the world it was necessary that it use the language of the world: that language was Greek.

Since the time of Alexander the Great the world had become increasingly Hellenised so far as language was concerned, and in the Roman period (in which Christ was born) Greek was spoken through the south of Europe into Asia Minor, and across into Africa and Egypt. In this unification of the world through a common tongue, it was not a local Greek dialect that was used, but the *koine* Greek.

Thus the New Testament was not written in a special "language of the Holy Spirit" but in the popular speech of the first century A.D. It made use of forceful words taken from the colloquial Greek of the market and the home, and such a language was ideal for the proclamation of the gospel to the uttermost parts of the world.

The Greeks prepared the world for this message by their gift of this language. Christian teachers found a store of already-prepared religious and philosophical expressions, especially those used by the translators of the Greek Septuagint Version of the Old Testament. The translators of the Jewish apocryphal books into Greek also helped to prepare for the New Testament revelation.

One Language, One Empire—One God!
The Scripture tells us that in the fulness of time God sent forth His Son for the salvation of the world, and in three special senses it was indeed "the fulness of time".

For instance, Alexander's conquests led to a universal unity of language, and the gospel would be proclaimed readily in every land.

Secondly, the establishment of the Roman empire meant that the nations of the world knew a political unity which at times protected this new faith. At first, the civil authorities hardly distinguished between Christians and Jews, and thus Christianity enjoyed the same privileges as Judaism, which was a protected religion under Roman law. In this connection, we may notice one of the purposes of the Acts of the Apostles —it was a defence, an 'apology' for the Christian faith.

Thirdly, the Jewish people had been dispersed far and wide, and the world now had knowledge of one true God—men were prepared for the revelation of the true monotheistic faith which Christianity proclaimed. It is strangely true that perhaps the greatest barriers to the gospel were raised by rigid Judaism, Greek philosophy, and, later, the pagan Roman government which could not understand Christ's supremacy, and yet the message was first preached in Jerusalem, the centre of Judaism; the language of its proclamation there, and throughout the first century world, was Greek; and the empire through which it spread was Roman.

One political empire, one universal tongue, the knowledge of one true God—these are all in the background of preparation as the fulness of time drew near, and then the Lord Jesus Christ was born. Those letters in Hebrew, Greek and Latin over the cross were a prophetic testimony to the ways in which the gospel of Jesus Christ would be published to the ends of the world, challenging to yet another unity—the oneness of all those who would be united into the family of God.

Not Pious Frauds!

In passing, it is worth noting that the chosen writers of these Gospels would hardly have been selected to foist a pious fraud on the world. Who would have chosen Matthew, a despised tax-gatherer? Or Mark, a servant who at one time failed in his commission as a Christian, or Luke, a doctor who probably never saw Jesus Christ in the flesh? Now that we know something of pseudepigraphy—writing under an assumed name —it is reasonable to assume that a pious fraud would have put out these writings in the name of the best-known Apostles. Humanly speaking, that would be more likely to lead to success than the choice of relatively unknown followers such as Mark and Luke. But this thing was of God, and no human effort could prevent its 'success'.

These inspired records have withstood the blasts of the centuries. They have not become lost in antiquity so that only fragments remain, but instead we have complete documents—as with the Old Testament documents too.

Four Pictures of Christ

In the chapters that follow we shall consider some of

the new light thrown on each of the Gospels. It is widely accepted that each Gospel writer gives a particular picture of the Lord Jesus Christ. These are not self-contained, nor does one picture exclude another, but in general Matthew presents Christ as King, Mark shows the Perfect Servant, Luke depicts the Man touched with the feelings of our infirmities, while John presents to us the eternal Son of God. These characteristics can be found in each of the Gospels, but the special emphasis in the particular Gospels is along these lines.

REFERENCE

[1]Deissmann, A. *Light From The Ancient East*, p. 73.

7

An Earthly Tax-Gatherer Writes About The Heavenly Kingdom

Matthew the tax-gatherer was especially chosen to present the story of the Man born to be King. His call is recorded at Matthew 9:9: "And as Jesus passed by from thence, He saw a man, called Matthew, sitting at the receipt of custom: and He saith unto him, Follow Me. And he arose, and followed Him."

The word for "receipt of custom" (*telōnion*) is in a papyrus letter from a young man named Polycrates, an obedient and industrious son who has concluded his religious duties and become apprenticed to a surveyor. He tells his father that he has sent a report of a certain site into the 'customs office'.

A Tax-Gatherer and a Zealot—Brothers In Christ
Matthew also records the call of other disciples, including Simon the Zealot (chapter 10:4).

An interesting side-light on our Lord's call of Matthew the tax-gatherer and of Simon the Zealot comes from an agreement among four tax-collectors, dating to A.D. 99. One clause was the acceptance of responsibility "for the salary of the sword-bearer". So opposed were the people to the tax-gatherers that these officials at times used the services of a Roman soldier —a sword-bearer.

Matthew would have been despised by his people, and especially by Zealots and other extreme groups pledged to violent opposition to the Romans. Some of them actually carried swords and sometimes used them against the overlords they hated. But when Christ said, "Follow Me", Matthew gave up the occupation that made him so objectionable to his own people, and Simon gave up his campaign of hatred against the Romans. Matthew and Simon had become brothers in Christ.

Illegal Extortion and Tax-Collecting Methods

Many petitions in New Testament times complain about the illegal extortion of the tax-gatherers. They were regarded as robbers, and orthodox Jews would not associate with such 'sinners'. This is the New Testament picture.

A typical petition comes from a weaver at Oxyrhynchus in A.D. 50. He complained that the tax-collector Apollophanes had extorted from him 16 drachmae of silver, and asked for proceedings to be instituted.

Apollophanes must have been quite a rogue, for another complaint, also dating to A.D. 50, tells us that "using great violence he seized from me a linen tunic which I was wearing, worth eight drachmae. He also extorted from me four more drachmae, and two drachmae each month during the six months from the month Neos Sebastos in the ninth year of Tiberius Claudius Caesar Augustus Germanicus Imperator of Pharmuthi; total, 24 drachmae. I therefore beg you to proceed against him as you may think fit."[1] In this second papyrus the petitioner refers to Apollophanes as "ex-collector of the trade tax upon weavers". Apparently he had been proceeded against and had lost his job.

One petition dating to A.D. 180 is against a tax-gatherer who had taxed a man over a period, on land which the man did not own. Eventually he realised what was going on and petitioned against the tax-collector. "I have incurred no small loss and it is unjust that I should be asked to pay the imposts on land which does not belong to me and which I do not cultivate," he claims, and asks for relief.[2]

The methods of the tax-collectors are indicated by the following letter from one: "You write to me about Hermodorus that I am too severe with him, for he is upsetting everything again. As for the cruelty of the collectors, I myself will be responsible for that . . ."[3]

The Romans continued the system which previous powers had followed— "farming the taxes". The government held an auction from time to time, and the rights of collecting taxes for a whole province were sold to the highest bidder. Often the sums involved were too great for one person to provide, and so monopolies developed, with wealthy people investing money in tax-collection.

Such a monopoly would in turn employ publicans, the tax-gatherers we meet so often in the New Testament. These men handed over a stipulated amount each year, but there was no adequate check on the actual taxes they collected. Thus they extorted as much as they could. As they were usually local people, they were hated by their fellow countrymen.[4]

The Kingdom "Suffers Violence"

Often the thinking of men was opposed to that of our Lord. This is well illustrated at Matthew 11:12, "The Kingdom of Heaven suffereth violence," the Greek word for "to suffer violence" being *biazomai*. While the meaning is somewhat obscure, it is used in the papyri to mean *compelled* or *pressed*. One man was being *pressed* by his friends to undertake a certain course of action, while another group were *compelled* to go to the threshing floor.

Possibly our Lord was suggesting that some were attempting to force the emergence of the Kingdom of God by *compelling* God to usher in His Kingdom in the special sense they hoped for. He went on to say that forceful men seize it—possibly referring to men such as the Zealots and the Sicarii (who were even more violently opposed to the rule of Rome). These were outside the will of God in attempting to set up the Kingdom of God by force. Even Peter's premature use of a sword was not condoned by our Lord. There was, then, a wrong *compulsion* by men who did not fully understand the purpose of Christ's coming. They did not comprehend that the Kingdom was to be ushered in in a new sense, with an emphasis on *spiritual* power. A change of attitude was required.

This change of attitude can be illustrated by our Lord's teaching on forgiveness. The disciples had to forgive, and not to hate, even when hatred seemed more logical. At Matthew 18 Peter came to the Lord and asked how often he should forgive his brother. Peter thought seven times was very generous, but our Lord told him he should forgive to seventy times seven. In other words, he should keep on forgiving.

Jesus then gave that great illustration of the man who was forgiven ten thousand talents by a king, and then had a fellow-servant thrown into prison until he could pay him a hundred pence. The man forgiven ten thousand talents—equivalent to about half a million dollars—would not forgive someone who owed him a sum amounting to a mere ten dollars. It was striking teaching about forgiveness—a teaching which our Lord demonstrated to the full when He cried on the cross, "Father, forgive them, for they know not what they do" (Luke 23:34). We feel very sorry for the poor man cast into prison, and so did his fellow-servants. At

Matthew 18:31 we read, "They were very sorry and came and told their lord all that was done." Their master put things right, and punished the one who had been so unforgiving.

The word used as the servants came to their master is *diesaphēsan*. It means more than 'told', for it has the idea of 'explain'. This is used in a papyrus letter dating to 168 B.C.,[5] from Isias to her husband urging him to return home from his monastic retreat. She writes:

> "When I got your letter from Horus, in which you *explained* that you were in retreat in the Serapeum at Memphis, I immediately gave thanks to the gods that you were well."

"Making a Reckoning"

Our Lord also said the king would "make a reckoning" with his servants. Until this century it was thought that this expression "make a reckoning" was unknown outside Bible writings. It is used again at Matthew 25:19 —the parable of the talents—where the absent lord eventually returned and *made a reckoning* with his servants. The papyrus from Oxyrhynchus has made it clear that this expression was known in New Testament times. In Papyrus No. 113 we have the phrase, ". . . that I may make a reckoning with him."

Another papyrus of the same collection is in the Berlin Museum, and it has a similarity to the story of the return of the lord who was making a reckoning with his servants. On that scrap is the phrase, ". . . until I come there and we make a reckoning."

A third use of the word is on an ostracon from Nubia, dated 6 March, A.D. 214, and again we have the expression "until the reckoning of the account". Little wonder that Adolf Deissmann and others who followed him after the turn of this century realised that these expressions demonstrated that the New Testament was indeed a Book written by people of New Testament times, originally intended for other people then living.

REFERENCES

[1] Grenfell, B. P., and Hunt, A. S. *The Oxyrhynchus Papyri*. Part II, p. 277, Oxy. Pap. No. 285, A.D. 50.
[2] Oxy. Pap. No. 718.
[3] Grenfell, B. P., and Hunt, A. S. *Ibid.*, p. 300, Oxy. Pap. No. 298, A.D. 1.
[4] Allen, I. *The Early Church And The New Testament*, pp. 54, 55.
[5] Papyrus British Museum 42.

8

New Light On
"The Sermon On
The Mount"

One of the best-known portions of Matthew's Gospel is the so-called "Sermon on the Mount", recorded at chapters 5–7. Others have written about the various theological interpretations of this 'sermon', but our special interest is in the new light thrown on the background from such sources as the recovered papyri.

However, perhaps it *is* relevant to say that we accept the traditional view that this was part of one address, given at one time, on the side of a Galilean hill. Probably much of the material was given at other times— it stands to reason that our Lord would repeat much of His teaching many times.

Salt—and Sodom and Gomorrah
In this "Sermon on the Mount" our Lord referred to salt. "Ye are the salt of the earth," He said, "But if the salt have lost his savour, wherewith shall it be salted?" (Matthew 5:13).

The salt used by the Jews came from the shores of the Dead Sea, alongside the area where it is believed the cities of Sodom and Gomorrah were once situated. A great area of salt, one hundred and fifty feet deep, runs for miles alongside those shores.[1]

Today, to the Arab the expression "became a pillar of salt" means the same as "frozen with fear" to the Englishman. Was the origin in the story of Lot's wife? For while it is not our purpose to tell the story of the destruction of Sodom and Gomorrah, it is relevant to mention that it is taken seriously today, even by non-Christian scholars. The various strata of the earth have been ruptured along the line of a great geological fault, and parts of them are still found, welded together by intense heat, high up on Jebel Usdum—the Arabic name for Mount Sodom. Pillars of salt are in the area today—one is forty feet high, and is called by the local people "Lot's Wife". We are not suggesting Lot's wife is inside, but if there can be such a pillar today, there could also be one of sufficient size to encase her when she rejected the grace of God and gazed back at the things she so reluctantly left. Her final disobedience in not 'hasting' (Genesis 19:22) brought the judgment she could have avoided.

Our Lord accepted this story as an actual happening, referring to the judgment on the cities (Matthew 11:23) and also pointedly warning, "Remember Lot's wife" (Luke 17:32). This is one of many Bible stories once regarded as legendary but now endorsed by modern scientific research.

Salt Under the Foot of Man
The Lord talked about salt being trodden under the feet of men. Salt was used in Jewish sacrifices (Leviticus 2:13), being added as a symbol of incorruption to every sacrifice. At Mark 9:49 the Lord says that "everyone shall be salted with fire, and every sacrifice shall be salted with salt." "Salt is good," He said, "But if the salt have lost his saltness, wherewith will ye season it?" The similar statement in the "Sermon on the Mount" is at Matthew 5:13: "Ye are the salt of the

earth: but if the salt have lost his savour, wherewith shall it be salted? It is thenceforth good for nothing, but to be cast out, and to be trodden under foot of men."

According to a Jewish tradition, when salt had become unfit for sacrificial use it was sprinkled in wet weather around the steps of the Temple so that the priests would not slip. Probably our Lord had this in mind as He used the local custom to portray a spiritual truth. Just as the sacrificial salt would be trodden under the feet of the priests, so those who lost their potential for service would, figuratively speaking, be trodden under the feet of men. How sad it is that in the history of the Church this has often happened! Many a man has been in Christian service, effective in presenting the incorruption which is in Jesus Christ, and then has lost his saltness—his savour of Christ. He is trodden under the feet of men.

The Candle Under a Bushel

Another point on which archaeology throws light is our Lord's statement at Matthew 5:15, "Neither do men light a candle and put it under a bushel but on a candlestick." The word our Lord used for 'bushel' is *modios*, and it actually means "a measure for things dry". It can apply to the quantity in the measure, or to the measure itself.

In the Australian Institute of Archaeology in Melbourne there is such a lampstand—or 'candlestick' as the Authorised Version of the Bible puts it—and it graphically illustrates this teaching of our Lord. The vessel is hollow, with a little shelf inside where the lamp can rest in the daytime. Thus the lamp is unlikely to be knocked off and broken by children. The vessel is sealed across the top, which thus forms an outside shelf on which the lamp can also be placed in the hours of darkness, able to give light to those in the house.

"An Eye for an Eye"—And a Second Mile

At Matthew 5:38 our Lord says, "Ye have heard that it hath been said, An eye for an eye, and a tooth for a tooth: But I say unto you, That ye resist not evil." This ancient law of Moses to which our Lord referred was not crude, as many would have us believe. It is not simply a law of retaliation, but is actually superior to the provisions of other ancient codes. In the famous Babylonian Code of Hammurabi penalties varied according to the social status of the offending party and the person who had been wronged. Where a slave would pay with his life, a nobleman would merely be fined.

When we come to the code of Moses, "An eye for an eye, and a tooth for a tooth" is clearly a pointer to equality of justice, something lacking even in the Code of Hammurabi which was the best of ancient law codes known outside the Bible.

Against the background of Moses' time "an eye for an eye" was remarkably just and humane. But our Lord went beyond Moses and told His disciples to "turn the other cheek" (Matthew 5:39).

This ideal is presented differently at Matthew 5:41, in "going the second mile". The Roman mile was 4,860 feet, or approximately twelve-thirteenths of an English mile. This was supposed to be one thousand paces in Roman times, and milestones showed distances from the large towns. In ancient times the Persians organised a postal system—especially from the days of Darius the Great—whereby government despatches were taken from stage to stage by forced messengers. This system was adopted by other peoples such as the Greeks and Romans, and this practice is referred to in Matthew

5:41: "And whosoever shall compel thee to go a mile, go with him twain."

A Roman official could force a non-Roman subject to carry any Roman's baggage for a mile along the highway, and Jesus was saying that His disciples should be prepared to go even two miles.

"Love Your Enemies"

The injunction in the same chapter, "Love your enemies," is an extension of the same principle, and this teaching is itself interesting against the background of Jewish history. At Matthew 5:43–45 we read, "Ye have heard that it hath been said, Thou shalt love thy neighbour, and hate thine enemy. But I say unto you, Love your enemies, bless them that curse you, do good to them that hate you, and pray for them which despitefully use you, and persecute you; that ye may be the children of your Father which is in heaven."

Our Lord said, "Ye have heard that it hath been *said* . . ." He was referring to an oral tradition, and not to the written law of Moses. The first part, "Thou shalt love they neighbour," was known to the Jews from the Laws of Moses, but the rabbis had added, "And hate thine enemy." Our Lord showed His rejection of the second clause and said instead, "Love your enemies."

We now know from the Dead Sea Scrolls that the Jews who lived out in the wilderness nurtured intense hatred against the Romans, and were taught to pursue their enemies ruthlessly and to destroy them without mercy. (See Chapter 3.)

Many of the Lord's listeners would know of these teachings, and we are reminded that He did not submit to the traditions of men, but brought His teachings back to the spiritual principles of the Kingdom of Heaven which He had come to announce. He went beyond "not hating" the enemy, and even said we should do good to those who hate us. In this way, He said, we would be the children of our Father in Heaven. This was in direct contrast to the teachings of "the sons of light"—as they called themselves—out in the wilderness.

Blowing One's Own Trumpet

Another comment in the "Sermon on the Mount" relates to the Jewish practice of having a trumpeter for certain formal processions. Jesus said, "Take heed that ye do not your alms before men, to be seen of them: otherwise ye have no reward of your Father which is in heaven. Therefore when thou doest thine alms, do not sound a trumpet before thee, as the hypocrites do in the synagogues and in the streets, that they may have glory of men. Verily I say unto you, They have their reward." (Matthew 6:1, 2). It is not difficult to see here the origin of the expression "blowing one's own trumpet" in the sense of praising oneself.

Jesus would have witnessed many processions from the synagogue. A trumpeter walked at the head of the procession, blowing his ram's horn. The officials of the synagogue followed, then came others, carrying the sacred box containing the scroll of the law. The procession wended its way to an open space in the town where a crowd waited. The box was set down and fine dust was sprinkled on it, then on the heads of the officials. Then the people sprinkled dust on their own heads, and they were urged by one of the elders to make sure this was not only sackcloth and ashes but true repentance.

The box was carried back to the synagogue, and those who were able gave alms to the poor. The rest of the day was supposed to be spent in fasting and prayer. Our Lord did not necessarily accede to these traditions, but taught that true almsgiving and practical goodness were not mere involvement with public display.

Further light from the Egyptian papyrus as to these verses in Matthew relates to the expression, "They have their reward." The Greek word for "to receive (as a reward)" is *apechō* and it is used in many papyri of New Testament times. It expresses in technical language that full payment has been made, and a receipt has been given.

One such receipt dating to A.D. 33 was issued at Thebes in ancient Egypt. Pamaris acknowledges the *receipt* of two drachmae from Abos, and here we have the New Testament word *apechō*. Another dates to A.D. 63, and is a *receipt for the full payment* of rent. The divorce deed of Paous and Tesenouphis makes it clear that the wife has received back the portion of the dowry owned by her husband. Each acknowledges that there will be no further claim against the other, and this returning of the dowry is *full payment*.

This aspect of someone receiving all he was entitled to is seen also at Luke 6:24 and Philippians 4:18.

As we apply this word *apechō* to the saying of our Lord, we realise that these hypocrites who blew trumpets to announce their almsgiving had "received their reward" in full—just as though they had been given a receipt and had no right to make any further claim.

Daily Bread . . . Bathing and Anointing
In this same chapter (Matthew 6) we have the so-called "Lord's prayer" which is a wonderful summary of principles to be followed in the believer's prayer life.

It might be surprising to know that one of the words unknown in Greek literature was the word 'daily', as when we pray, "Give us this day our *daily* bread" (Matthew 6:11). The word is *epiousion*, and this also was found in the Fayum area of Egypt, in the record of a housekeeper's account. It meant "a daily allowance of food".

Implied in our Lord's teaching is the truth that the needs of *today* are brought before God in this special sense.

Another verse on which the papyrus throws light relates to our Lord's statement at Matthew 6:17, "But thou, when thou fastest, anoint thine head, and wash thy face." The custom of bathing and anointing is touched on in one of these ancient papyrus letters where a man writes that his whole way of life is out of routine because his wife is absent on a visit. So he writes, "I never bathed or anointed myself from July 12 to August 12."

Yet another man was away from home and his house was robbed. He wanted to know more about it, so he wrote to his wife, "I shall not even wash myself till I hear the news."

Our Lord's expression concerning anointing and washing clearly fits the background of the times, and the spiritual lesson was that such a practice—i.e. fasting—should not simply be for the purpose of displaying oneself before men. This is an essential teaching as to the Kingdom of Heaven, for the believer's commendation is primarily from God rather than men.

On Pulling Out Splinters

Our Lord demonstrated a sense of humour in His saying in Matthew 7:3, 4 when He said: "And why beholdest thou the mote that is in thy brother's eye, but considerest not the beam that is in thine own eye? Or how wilt thou say to thy brother, Let me pull out the mote out of thine eye; and, behold, a beam is in thine own eye?"

It is just as though someone with a branch of a tree sticking out of his eye stopped his friend and said, "Let me pull that splinter out of your eye!"

We saw in Chapter 1 that the first clue as to the importance of the findings of Drs. Grenfell and Hunt at Oxyrhynchus was when Dr. Hunt noticed the word 'mote' on a crumpled piece of papyrus. It was soon recognised that this was one of the famous *Logia*, the so-called "Sayings of Jesus".*

There are various other pictures that could be painted from the "Sermon of the Mount", such as the linking of bad trees with bad fruit at Matthew 7:17. Here again our Lord was using phraseology current in the days of His ministry in Palestine.

The Two Houses

As He concluded this address our Lord told a story of two houses. Those who heard His words and put His teachings into practice were like a man whose house was built on a rock, able to withstand the rain, the floods, and the wind. Those who heard His words, but did *not* apply them in living, were like the foolish man who built his house on the sand, and it was soon destroyed.

The word here translated 'rain' is the Greek word *brochē*, and this was supposed to be a word unknown in Bible times apart from its use in the New Testament. But the Oxyrhynchus papyri have changed all that. One papyrus dealing with a lease of land refers to an inundation,[2] and dates to A.D. 88–89. A contract is based on a four years' lease, with the proviso that in that time there are four inundations—in several other leases it is made clear that any year in which the inundation does not take place is not counted as a year. Our special point of interest is this use of the Greek word *brochē* as in Matthew 7. The New Testament usage is again confirmed as being part of the living language of those times.

*See Chapter 4.

REFERENCES

[1] Beasley, W. J. *The Amazing Story Of Sodom*, pp. 21, 22, referring to Professor M. Kyle's book, *Explorations at Sodom*.

[2] Oxy. Pap. No. 280.

9

Mark: "The Common People Heard Him Gladly"

We have seen that the findings from the mummified crocodiles of Egypt led to the conclusion that the New Testament was written in the language of everyday people, and we have also referred to the statement at Mark 12:37, "The common people heard him gladly". This does not mean 'common' in the sense of rude or undesirable persons, but simply 'the man in the street' —those who in a previous generation would have been called the middle and lower classes.

As this is especially the claim of Mark, we shall see some of the ways in which the papyri illustrate his use of words understood by "the common people".

Clothed and in His Right Mind

Even the Greek word *himatizō*, "I clothe", was claimed to be known only in Biblical writings, such as Mark 5:15. There we read of a man who had been possessed with a legion of demons now seated, clothed, and in his right mind. It seems strange that scholars of only a century ago should have thought that primitive Christians would need to invent a new word in the Bible to talk about someone being 'clothed', and not surprisingly the word has now been found in a document dating to 163 B.C. It is also used in the Oxyrhynchus papyri, in a document dating to A.D. 117, in the testament of a man named Dionysius the son of Harpocration. There are two references to the children of a family slave who had been fed and *clothed* by the wife of the testator—and the word for 'clothed' is the same as in Mark 5.

Another document which uses this word is an instrument of adoption, dated to 31 December, A.D. 301. The man being adopted states he will feed and clothe his benefactor nobly, as though he were "a proper and natural son". Again we have the same word for 'clothe' as in Mark 5.

Two by Two

In the next chapter, at Mark 6:7, we read that Jesus sent forth His disciples *duo duo*—"two by two". Dr. Adolf Deissmann makes this statement:

> "A distributive numeral relation is here expressed in the Greek by repeating the cardinal number. Wellhausen (In 'Das Evangelium Marci übersetzt und erklärt', Berlin, 1903, p. 52) says that this is not truly Greek—but it is found in Aeschylus and Sophocles. These examples would be sufficient to account for the same use in the Septuagint and in the New Testament; it agrees with the Semitic use, it is true, but it is good popular Greek for all that."[1]

Illustrating this New Testament use of numbers, Dr. Deissmann gives an example from the third century A.D., quoting Oxyrhynchus Papyrus No. 121 in which a man named Isidorus writes to another named Aurelius to "bind the branches three by three in bundles". Here "three by three" is *tria tria*, just as *duo duo* is "two by two" in the New Testament usage.

This particular letter also includes the expression "bind them in bundles", as in the parable of the good seed and the tares in Matthew 13.

Take No Scrip

Another interesting point from archaeology relates to

the word 'scrip' at Mark 6:8 (also at Matthew 10:10 and Luke 9:3). In the Revised Version this word is 'wallet', and most commentators have tended to think of this either as a travelling bag or a bag in which to keep bread. The word in Greek is *pēra* and *could* mean either a travelling bag or a bread bag, but we know from an ancient monument that it also had another special meaning. This monument was erected in the Roman period at Kefr-hauar, in Syria, by a man who regarded himself as a slave of a Syrian goddess. He went begging on her behalf, and he boasts that on each journey he "brought in seventy *bags*". Once again the word is *pēra*. It does not apply to provision bags, nor to travelling bags, but it was the beggar's collecting bag.

The travelling friar of the Middle Ages had such a bag, and the triangular piece of material hanging from behind the left shoulder of a junior barrister's gown was originally a wallet in which his fees were put. These were later developments associated with this 'wallet'.

Our Lord was showing His disciples that they were *not* to carry such a wallet—in other words, they were not to go out as beggars. Other religions in ancient times had their beggar priests, but this was not to be the practice of those who followed the true God.

In another letter we find further light on this same chapter, Mark 6. A man writes that there is hardly a single plot that the water will irrigate. This word 'plot' (*prasia*) actually refers to a garden bed, and is the word used at Mark 6:40: "And they sat down in ranks, by hundreds, and by fifties." The word 'ranks' is this same word—it seems that the groups looked like a lot of garden beds spread around the green grass (v. 39).

"The String of His Tongue was Loosed"
At Mark 7 we have the story of the healing of a deaf

and dumb man, and at verse 35 is a comment that at first seems difficult: "And straightway his ears were opened, and the bond of his tongue was loosed." In an attempt to make sense of the expression the translators of the Authorised Version made it "the string of his tongue", but the word literally is 'bond'.

This expression, "the bond of his tongue", has usually been taken to be some sort of figurative language, but it is actually a technical phrase, relating to a man who is bound by demonic influences. As early as the fourth century B.C. the expression is used, on a tablet found at Attica—it is a petition to the gods against a man's enemies. After listing a whole group of men he wants harmed, he says, "I *bind* these all down to Hermes, who is beneath the earth and crafty and fast-holding and luck-bringing, and I will not loose them."[2] There the word 'bind' is a verb form, whereas 'bond' in the Bible phrase ("the bond of his tongue") is a noun form.

Another of these magical inscriptions has a bitter cursing against a man's enemy,

> "*Bound* and fast held be the mouth and fast held the tongue of curses, of vows, and of invocations of the gods ... *Bound* be the tongue in its mouth, fast held be its lips, shaken, fettered, and banned the teeth, and stopped the ears of curses and invocations."[3]

At Luke 13:16 our Lord stated that Satan had 'bound' a daughter of Abraham for eighteen years. This woman had a spirit of infirmity, and her 'bond' was released by Jesus one Sabbath day.

Putting these aspects together, it seems that our story in Mark where the dumb man was made to speak tells us, not only that the mute was able to talk, but also that Satanic chains of darkness were snapped. The man was given a new freedom by Jesus Christ.

The Picturesque Style of the East
Our Lord used the eastern style of those around Him.

In this connection it is interesting to read one papyrus fragment dating to about the middle of the second century A.D.[4] This is actually a quotation from the famous Greek philosopher Aristotle who had lived over four centuries before. These words are put in the mouth of Aristotle:

> "We do not consider a bad horse to be of any value if it has gold chains and costly trappings; we rather give our praise to one that is in sound condition. Besides what we have said, too, worthless persons, when they obtain wealth and value their possessions more than the goods of the soul, are in the worst case of all."

Our Lord used somewhat similar language when He rebuked the Pharisees because they were concerned with the appearance of the outside of the cup and not with the cleanliness of the inside. They would whitewash sepulchres and forget that actually they were tombs full of dead men's bones. The Lord also talked of a man's soul being of more value than all the things of the earth—"for what shall a man give in exchange for his soul?" (Mark 8:37).

His approach was infinitely superior to that of Aristotle. In the papyrus before us the philosopher merely goes on to suggest that a man ought to find satisfaction within his own nature and seek for the acquisition of knowledge. Our Lord showed the need of a new nature and of a new knowledge. He did not merely present a philosophy for this life, but taught men how to enter the very Kingdom of God itself. He was not merely a philosopher; He was God incarnate, and the Saviour of the world.

A Millstone Around the Neck

At Mark 9:42 the Lord warned against offending one of the little ones who believed in Him. "It would be better," He said, "That a millstone were hanged about his neck, and that he were thrown into the sea."

The word for millstone here is *onikos* and it literally means "belonging to an ass". It is used only here, and in the same context again at Matthew 18:6. This also was included in J. H. Thayer's list of strictly 'Biblical' words, but the word is in a document dated to 8 February, A.D. 33, specifically mentioning "the *ass* and her foal".

In another document from Egypt, dating to 5 February, A.D. 70, there is reference to the loan of an *ass*—we are even told it was a mouse-coloured ass! The point we are making is that the New Testament usage is entirely in accordance with the times. We have seen that the New Testament form of the word does not necessarily mean an ass as such but it was also used to refer to the ass's burden, or to what belonged to an ass. A colloquial expression developed— this word *onikos* became a synonym for a millstone, as in the Gospels of Matthew and Mark. (Luke used a different word, simply referring to a stone as such.)

An old Jewish proverb has developed around the millstone. It says that a man may marry, and after that he may dedicate himself to the study of the law; but, says the proverb, by his marriage he dedicates himself to the study of the law with a millstone about his neck. Perhaps not all modern lawyers or religious leaders would agree with that adage!

Destroying someone by putting a millstone around his neck (see Mark 9:42) was not a means of execution accepted by Jewish law, but it was occasionally used by the Greeks.

A Spiritual Baptism

At Mark 10:38 our Lord told His disciples of the spiritual baptism He faced, and asked, "Can ye drink of the cup that I drink of? And be baptised with the baptism that I am baptised with?" This word 'baptism' does not only apply to the ceremony whereby a person is immersed in water, and indeed in the New Testament itself it is also used concerning hands that are unwashed—at Mark 7:4 we read, "And when they come from the market, except they wash, they eat not. And many other things there be, which they have received to hold, as the washing of cups, and pots, brasen vessels, and of tables." The word for 'washing' (literally 'washings') is the usual word for 'baptised'—the cups were immersed for their washing.

The word is also used in a letter from Apollonius to his father.[5] When everything was going wrong he wrote that, even when it seemed he was about to be delivered, "just then we are *immersed* in trouble." Apollonius was baptised, immersed, in trouble.

These then are some of the ways in which Mark makes it clear that "the common people heard Him gladly". And we of the twentieth century continue to listen, for Jesus Christ speaks to the "common people" of all ages.

REFERENCES

[1]Deissmann, A. *Light From The Ancient East*, pp. 124, 125.
[2]*Ibid.*, p. 307.
[3]*Ibid.*, p. 308.
[4]Grenfell, B. P., and Hunt, A. S. *The Oxyrhynchus Papyri*. Part IV, p. 85, Oxy. Pap. No. 666.
[5]Milligan, G. *Selections From The Greek Papyri*, p. 22, Paris Pap. No. 47, c. 153 B.C.

10
Stories Of Jesus In Luke

Some of the most 'human' New Testament writings are in the Gospel of Luke. We have said that Luke especially presents Christ as the Son of Man, and this doctor of the first century A.D. was equipped for this by his understanding of human nature.

Writing to Theophilus

Luke begins by telling us that many *"had taken in hand"* the setting forth of the gospel story. This same word is used in a petition to the Prefect of Oxyrhynchus.[1] Syrus 'endeavoured' to carry off the lad Apion into slavery, "having endeavoured" in the papyrus being the same word as "taken in hand" at Luke 1. It implies that a commencement had been made.

In this same papyrus document we find a word used at Hebrews 13:19. The writer asked the brethren to pray that he might be 'restored' to them the sooner. The word 'restored' is *apokatastathō*, and in this papyrus we find that Apion was 'restored' to his parents by order of the Prefect. Syrus is the same as Pesouris— he had earlier carried off this boy and had been ordered to return him, but apparently had not obeyed the court's injunction.

It is interesting also to notice that Luke's record was primarily a letter—"It seemed good to me ... to write unto thee in order, most excellent Theophilus", we read at Luke 1:3.

'Theophilus'—which means "lover of God"—is a common enough name of those times, and it turns up in the papyri—not the same man, but another of the same name. There are many other examples of New Testament names being used in this way—for instance Epaphroditus, Dionysius, and Trophimus.

Martha was "Cumbered About"
Another word which reminds us of New Testament usage is *perispaō*. "I entreat you for her sake and for ours to return to the city, unless indeed something most pressing *occupies* you."[2] This is a derivative of the word used of Martha at Luke 10:40—she was cumbered about, or distracted, with much serving. She was, in fact, 'occupied' with much serving. As in the papyrus letter before us, this *serving* was in one sense a hindrance, preventing her full appreciation of the privilege of worship. She let it affect her attitude.

The husband in this letter was also 'occupied'—in his case with religious engagements, for he was too busy to care for his starving wife and family.

The Good Samaritan
The story of the Good Samaritan is recorded at Luke 10. It is a masterpiece, told in only thirteen verses (vs. 25–37). Here is part of it:

> "And Jesus answering said, A certain man went down from Jerusalem to Jericho, and fell among thieves, which stripped him of his raiment, and wounded him, and departed, leaving him half dead.
> And by chance there came down a certain priest that way: and when he saw him, he passed by on the other side.
> And likewise a Levite when he was at the place, came and looked on him, and passed by on the other side.
> But a certain Samaritan as he journeyed, came where he was, and when he saw him, he had compassion on him,

And went to him, and bound up his wounds, pouring in oil and wine, and set him on his own beast, and brought him to an inn, and took care of him . . ."

Now follows a complaint by two pig merchants, dating to A.D. 171:

"Yesterday, which was the 19th of the present month Thoth, as we were returning about daybreak from the village of Theadelphia in the division of Themistes, certain malefactors came upon us between Polydeucia and Theadelphia, and bound us and also the guard of the tower, and assaulted us with very many stripes, and wounded Pasion, and robbed us of one pig, and carried off Pasion's coat . . ."

Several parallels are obvious. In both records we read of the road on which the robbery took place. We are told about the stripes by which the men were beaten, and we are sorry to hear that even the clothing of one was stolen. The papyrus shows that our Lord's story had as its basis the kind of occurrence which was probably quite familiar to His hearers.

Buying and Selling Sparrows
At Luke 12:6 we read, "Are not *five sparrows* sold for *two farthings*, and not one of them is forgotten before God?" But when we go to Matthew 10:29 we hear our Lord say, "Are not *two sparrows* sold for *a farthing?*" This indicates that one received a greater quantity at a discount price—and this was true in ancient times as it is today.

An edict, known as the maximum tariff, comes from the time of the Roman emperor Diocletian. It tells of the highest price at which various items can be sold, and four sparrows are included. Thus in this edict dating to the third century A.D. we find that sparrows are the cheapest of all birds used for foods—even cheaper than starlings. At that time ten sparrows were to be sold for no more than sixteen denarii, this being a new copper coin and not the silver denarius of the New Testament.

The point we are making is that the Lord Jesus Christ was talking about an actual condition, where sparrows were sold on the open market. He was using His own background as a starting point for wonderful spiritual teaching. Even a sparrow's lot was noticed by God, and the Lord went on to say that every man was worth far more than a sparrow.

Giving Right Judgment

Another apt lesson of our Lord related to the signs of nature. The Jewish people could discern the weather—when they saw a cloud rising in the west they immediately said, "A shower of rain is coming". When there was a south wind blowing they said, "It will be scorching heat". "You hypocrites," said the Lord Jesus Christ, "You know how to interpret these matters relating to the earth and the heavens, but you cannot interpret what is taking place in front of your eyes."

We have translated freely, but that is the meaning of what our Lord said at Luke 12:56. He went on to illustrate His teaching in these words:

"Yea, and why even of yourselves judge ye not what is right? When thou goest with thine adversary to the magistrate, as thou art in the way, *give diligence* that thou mayest be delivered from him; lest he hale thee to the judge, and the judge deliver thee to the officer, and the officer cast thee into prison. I tell thee, thou shalt not depart thence, till thou has paid the very last mite." (Luke 12:57–59).

Here again the papyrus has given us light. It was said that this word 'diligence' was virtually unknown outside the Bible, but now it has been found in a Senate decree dating to 81 B.C. in which there is a plea, "May

89

they take heed and give diligence"—the latter expression being the same as in Luke 12:58.

It also occurs in the Oxyrhynchus papyri in a letter dating to 2 B.C. Thus this expression which was thought to be a stiff and formal translation turns out to be part of the living language of the people of New Testament times.

In that same passage there is another expression on which the papyrus gives illumination—where our Lord says "Why judge ye not what is right?" This also was thought to be unique to the New Testament, but it has been found in an inscription which proves to be a prayer to the goddess Demeter, pleading for vengeance and imploring her to give *right judgment*.

"Hear, goddess, and give *right judgment*," asks the supplicant—and in doing so he reminds us that this expression was known outside the Bible. Our Lord used it in this practical advice to those who would go to law with each other. He urged them to be reconciled before such a judgment by a magistrate was given. Rather, they should end their dispute by themselves pronouncing "right judgment".

In one papyrus document[3] a petitioner Philumene is seeking the return of two thousand drachmae she had lent to another woman. However, the court is not asked for the money only, but also for the penalties incurred through non-payment. This is outlined as the "penalty of paying us in full any loss or damage which we might incur in connection with the transaction, in addition to half the amount with the other guarantees contained in the agreement."[4]

We have already seen that sometimes half the amount was added as well as interest on repayments. Perhaps law costs were as heavy in those days as sometimes they are today!

The relevance to our Lord's lesson is clear. These people who heard His teaching understood signs all around them in the material world, but could not recognise the clear spiritual signs. A day of reckoning was coming, and they should avoid the judgment of the 'Magistrate', even God Himself, when the Heavenly courts of law were finally set up.

The Lost Sheep

Several papyri[5] contain registers of sheep and goats pastured; they compare numbers with previous years, and they follow a set formula. Clearly the shepherds were expected to give proper returns.

One letter dating to A.D. 23[6] tells of a slave named Cerinthus who reports that he intends to transfer his sheep to another district on the other side of the river.

Yet another return dating to A.D. 26 is addressed to an official by two people who tell how many sheep they own in the twelfth year of Tiberius,[7] while the next papyrus in this collection is dated to A.D. 66.[8] The sender registers an additional seven lambs, these having been born since the previous return for the current year. Not only was it necessary to account for sheep actually owned, but even details about additional lambs had to be recorded. Another return dating to A.D. 1 makes it clear that the State imposed a tax on sheep.

All this is interesting to set against the story of the lost sheep. A secondary economic motive is in the background to the story. This is perhaps even more significant when we find (at Luke 15:1) that "all the tax-gatherers" came around and listened to this story. That lost sheep was valuable, and it must be accounted for, not only to the owner's satisfaction, but also to the tax-assessor's!

Leprosy . . . and the Ten Lepers

Luke has a special interest in medical matters such as

leprosy, and another of his stories is that of the ten lepers (Luke 17:12–19).

An indication of the prevalence of leprosy comes from a declaration on oath, dating to A.D. 77, concerning the sale of an eight-year-old slave girl.[9] The contract says that this girl Sarapous is the property of a woman Bacche, and it says of the slave that she "is about eight years old and without blemish apart from epilepsy and leprosy". This does not imply that she suffered from epilepsy or leprosy, but such a clause is regularly found in contracts for the sale of slaves. It meant they were not guaranteed as free from these two complaints which were so prevalent in the world of the New Testament.

In passing it surely is sad to realise that here was a little girl who could be so callously sold from person to person. Her owner even declared that young Sarapous was not mortgaged.

"Only this Stranger . . ."
The ten lepers to whom Luke referred met the Lord and from a distance cried out, "Jesus, Master, have mercy on us." Christ told them to show themselves to the priests and, when they obeyed and went, they were cleansed. One of the ten, seeing he was healed, turned back and glorified God. He fell down at the feet of the Lord and gave Him thanks—and the man was a Samaritan. (Elsewhere in the Scriptures—at John 4:9—we are reminded that the Jews had no dealings with the Samaritans.*)

Then follow those memorable words of the Lord Jesus Christ:

"And Jesus answering said, Were there not ten cleansed? But where are the nine? There are not found

---

*John 4:9 is now known to mean "The Jews do not use (vessels) together with Samaritans" (cf. New English Bible).

that returned to give glory to God, save this stranger. And He said unto him, Arise, go thy way: thy faith hath made thee whole."

The word our Lord used here for 'stranger' is *allogenēs*, and it means "of another race", or 'foreigner'. Before the papyrus findings of relatively recent times it was considered that this word was known only in the Greek Septuagint version of the Old Testament, and here in Luke 17:18. It was recognised that those who wrote about the Bible used the word, but it was claimed it was not known in other writings. However, it was actually used in the inscription on the Inner Court of the Temple at Jerusalem.

Scholars differ as to whether this inscription (which was discovered in 1871) would have been put up by Roman or Jewish authorities, but it was certainly meant to be read by Gentiles. It was they who, by this notice, were threatened with death as the penalty for going beyond the warning point. The inscription stated that no *foreigner* could pass beyond the enclosure around the sanctuary, and anyone who did so would be responsible for his own death that would follow.

Here we have the same word our Lord used about the one man—the 'stranger'—who returned to give thanks. Clearly the Gentiles knew the meaning of the word, and although our Lord could have used other more specifically Jewish words, He chose a word that was understood by any Gentiles who witnessed this healing of one of their own number. Even a 'foreigner' could enjoy blessing from the Christ of God.

Two Widows—Hitting Under the Eye and Two Mites
Luke also records the parable of the widow who asked the judge to avenge her. The judge would not listen to her pleas, but then he says to himself, "Though I fear not God, nor regard man; yet because this widow

troubleth me, I will avenge her, lest by her continual coming she weary me" (Luke 18:4, 5). This word 'weary' is in Greek *hupōpiazō*, and it has the general idea of "hitting under the eye"—to be buffeted, as in prize fighting. No wonder the judge was prepared to listen to the voluble lady in our Lord's parable!

As Dr. Deissmann says in this connection, "The papyri and inscriptions furnish good contemporary illustrations of our Lord's parables—e.g. the importunate widow at Luke 18:1ff."*

Yet another word that was supposed not to be known was the Greek word *perisseia*, meaning 'abundance'. In the "Imperial Period" of Roman rule, one particular president of the athletic games gave over to the city the *surplus money* that traditionally belonged to him as president. Another inscription, from Syria, dating to A.D. 329, also refers to superfluous funds.

In the New Testament the word is used many times, as at Luke 21:4 in the lovely story of the widow who gave two mites to the Jewish treasury. She gave her all—the rich men merely gave of their *surplus funds*; and so their giving was no sacrifice whatever.

This same word is used at Romans 5:17 to remind us that we shall receive *abundance* of grace. God's gifts to us are overflowing—they cannot be contained by human measure. The practical outworking of this is shown at II Corinthians 8:2 where we read of those in the churches of Macedonia who had had a great trial of affliction, but despite their extreme poverty they knew an *abundance* of joy—an overflowing joy which could not be measured by human standards.

REFERENCES

[1]Milligan, G. *Selections From The Greek Papyri*, p. 52, Oxy. Pap. No. 38, A.D. 49–50.

Light From The Ancient East, p. 131, footnote.

[2] *Ibid.*, p. 11, British Museum Papyrus 42, B.C. 168.
[3] Grenfell, B. P., and Hunt, A. S. *The Oxyrhynchus Papyri.* Part II, p. 278, Oxy. Pap. No. 286, A.D. 82.
[4] *Ibid.*
[5] For example, Grenfell, B. P., and Hunt, A. S. *Ibid.*, p. 310, Oxy. Pap. No. 354.
[6] *Ibid.*, p. 194, Oxy. Pap. No. 244.
[7] *Ibid.*, Oxy. Pap. No. 245.
[8] *Ibid.*, p. 195, Oxy. Pap. No. 246.
[9] *Ibid.*, p. 234, Oxy. Pap. No. 263, A.D. 77.

11

The Prodigal Son

One famous papyrus letter has been compared with the story of the Prodigal Son in Luke 15, and this is how Dr. Deissmann translated it:

"Antonis Longus to Nilus his mother many greetings. And continually do I pray that thou art in health. I made supplication for thee daily to the lord Serapis. I would thou shouldst understand that I had no hope that thou wouldst go up to the metropolis. And therefore I came not to the city. But I was ashamed to come to Caranis, because I walk about in rags. I write (or 'have written') to thee that I am naked. I beseech thee, mother, be reconciled to me. Furthermore, I know what I have brought upon myself. I have been chastened every way. I know that I have sinned. I have heard from Postumus, who met thee in the country about Arsinoe and out of season told thee all things."[1]

Then Antonis tells his mother that he would rather become a cripple than owe anybody anything at all! At that point the letter breaks off into fragments which include such expressions as "Come yourself" . . . "I beseech you" . . ., and then again, "I beseech you."

This runaway son has been involved in loose living and has piled up many debts. He fares badly in the far country, and his clothes are falling off in rags. Just as in the Bible story, he feels he cannot go home and yet he must. He recognises that all his troubles are the result of his own folly. He longs to be restored to fellowship with his mother, and while in this state he meets the man Postumus who in turn had met his mother.

Will Mother Pay His Debts?

Obviously the son knows that the mother's love is great, for there is a suggestion that she should pay his debts so that he will not owe anything to anybody. He earnestly beseeches her to come herself to recover him, and his expressions are similar to those of the New Testament story. Some might suggest he was but a hypocrite, imposing on his loving mother. But the other side is that he is sensible enough to know how different his state is from what it had been.

"I was ashamed," Antonis wrote, "I know that I have sinned." In similar language the Prodigal in Luke says, "I have sinned ... I am no longer worthy to be called your son."

"I walk about in rags," the pathetic letter from Egypt states. "Bring forth the best robe and put it on him!" orders the father in the New Testament story.

"I beseech thee, mother, be reconciled to me," pleads the lonely disillusioned wanderer in Egypt. "I will arise and go to my father," determines the young man of Luke 15. Was *he* reconciled? Of course! We read at verse 20, "But when he was yet a great way off his father saw him, and had compassion, and ran, and fell on his neck, and kissed him."

We have seen that Antonis tells his mother that he "makes prayer for her daily" to his god Serapis. This is the same expression which the Apostle Paul uses when he tells the Christians at Ephesus that he makes continuous mention of them in his prayers (Ephesians 1:16). This is a good example of the way the Bible writers use the language of their times to enrich and ennoble it. If the words were not in the style of the day we would suspect their genuineness, but we are delighted to find that that authenticity cannot be challenged, and that a new and noble dimension is added: for Paul's prayers are directed to the one true God, to the one who hears and answers prayer.

A Plea for Reconciliation

Another illustration of this principle is in this same letter, for no less than three times we read that Antonis used the words *parakalō sai*—"I beseech thee". This is a verb form of the word in I John 2:1, *paraklētos*. There we read, "If any man sin, we have an *advocate* with the Father, Jesus Christ the righteous." This can be linked with our Lord's promise at John 14:16, "I will pray the Father, and He shall give you another *Comforter*, that He may abide with you for ever." The word is *paraklētos*—the strengthener, one called alongside to help.

The usage is interesting. Antonis acknowledges to his mother, "I have sinned", and here again there is a connection with our verse at I John 2:1. For Antonis uses another form of the word 'sin' that is used in the injunction by the aging Apostle John—"If we *sin*, we have an *advocate*." We do not know whether this prodigal son's beseeching led to a reconciliation with his mother, but we do know that the Scripture is true: and we are assured therein that we have a Beseecher, an Advocate. As our sins are confessed, they are forgiven and we are reconciled with our Father.

There are other common words in this letter which are used in the New Testament. Antonis writes about Postumus who "out of season" told his mother all about his waywardness. The Apostle Paul used this word at II Timothy 4:2 as he urged young Timothy, "Preach the word, be instant in season and *out of season.*"

When Antonis said he would rather be maimed than *owe* anything to anybody, he used the same word *opheiletēs* that the Apostle used at Romans 1 : 14 where he says, "I am *debtor* both to the Greeks, and to the barbarians; both to the wise, and to the unwise". Again Paul uses the word at Galatians 5 : 3 when he says that he who is in bondage to the law is a *debtor* to do the whole law. This is yet a further example of an everyday word becoming a word full of spiritual significance. Christ has forgiven us our sins, and we are no longer "in debt" to the law. We have been forgiven much, and we in turn have become willing slaves in the cause of Him who redeemed us. We are *debtors* to preach the gospel.

Another word on which this papyrus letter throws light is 'reconciled'. As Antonis begs his mother to be reconciled to him, he uses the word *diallassō*. Our Lord used this word at Matthew 5:24: a man should first be reconciled to his brother before offering a gift at the altar. It was a strong word that the Lord used, having the idea of "changing thoroughly"—it even has the thought of conciliating the one who has been sinned against. Not only will this 'reconciliation' involve a different attitude towards our brother, but will also mean that our offering to God is accepted. As our hearts are right with our brethren, so they are right before God.

Perhaps rather fortunately this letter from ancient Egypt is dated to the second century A.D., and so quite clearly was written after the story of the Prodigal Son in Luke 15. Dr. Deissmann has an interesting comment as a footnote:

> "If this letter had happened to be preserved in some literary work there would of course be a number of monographs, proving the parable to be derived from the letter, and many a doctoral dissertation would have been made out of it."[2]

Music and Feasting

There are touches from other ancient letters which also help us to see this story of the Prodigal Son as a product of those times. One letter dating to 245 B.C., found in the wrappings of a mummy in the Necropolis of El-Hibeh in ancient Egypt, gives instructions as to the preparations for a forthcoming feast. Musicians are to be hired, and clothing is to be provided for the womenfolk. Demophon is obviously a wealthy Egyptian and he goes on to write, "And fetch also the kid from Aristion and send it to us." This no doubt was to provide the meat to be roasted for the great festival. We see in this letter an echo of the loving words of the Prodigal's father, "Bring forth the best robe, and put it on him . . . And bring hither the fatted calf, and kill it: and let us eat, and be merry" (verses 22, 23). It reminds us too of what the older son had to say about the rejoicing at the return of the Prodigal. "These many years have I served you," he complained to his father, "But you never gave me a kid that I might make merry with my friends!" (Luke 15:29).

"The Portion that Falls to Me"

Yet another touch comes from an Egyptian landowner named Asclepiades to his tenant Portis, "I have received from thee the fruit that *falleth to me*," and this is the same colloquial expression—*epiballein*—as in the story of the Prodigal Son where the younger son says, "Father, give me the portion that *falls to me*" (Luke 15:12).

The word is also found in a petition by a tax-gatherer, dated to 117 B.C.[3] This tax-gatherer is anxious to gain the good graces of Amenneus, the royal scribe, and he frankly says he is "eager to be a member of your house because it chiefly *falls to you* to look after the interests of the Crown".

There are various other interesting expressions in this

particular letter, such as the recognition that the inhabitants of the village *"with one accord"* looked to this royal scribe for protection. This expression is the same as at Acts 1:14 where the Christians "continued *with one accord* in prayer and supplications".

One final word used in both the story of the Prodigal Son and the papyri is that for "riotous living". This word is used at Luke 15:13, and derivatives of it are also found at Ephesians 5:18, Titus 1:6, and I Peter 4:4. In one papyrus document[4] a young man's parents publicly announce they will no longer be responsible for their son's debts incurred through his "riotous living" (*asōteuomenos*).

We see, then, that many words from the papyrus documents of Egypt assure us that the story of the Prodigal Son was indeed set against the background of New Testament times. Luke's careful recording of historical events—as has been demonstrated so clearly in relation to the Acts of the Apostles[5]—is seen also in his Gospel presentation. His account of stories told by the Lord Jesus Christ bear the hall-marks of authenticity. They 'breathe' the very atmosphere of those times.

REFERENCES

[1]Deissmann, A. *Light From The Ancient East*, p. 177.
[2]*Ibid.*
[3]Milligan, G. *Selections From The Greek Papyri*, p. 27, Tebtunis Pap. No. 40.
[4]*Ibid.*, pp. 71, 72, Florentine Pap. No. 99, A.D. 1–2.
[5]See, for example, Ramsay, Sir William. *The Bearing Of Recent Discoveries On The Trustworthiness Of The New Testament*, ch. 6.

12

The Son Of God In
John's Gospel

In John's Gospel there are clear statements as to the Deity of the Lord Jesus Christ. In a special sense this Gospel presents to us Him who is and always was the Son of the living God. Thus at John 2 we find He could turn water to wine—so demonstrating His omnipotence. John deliberately selects signs such as this to show forth the Deity of Christ. He shows Him as the one who can give sight to a man born blind, and as the one who could even raise the dead. He is the *Logos*, the Word of God, the one who has exegeted (or fully revealed) the Father (John 1:18).

Talking to a Woman in Samaria
At John 4 our Lord is talking to a woman at a well near the ancient Israelite capital of Samaria. "You worship you know not what," He said, and then, at verse 23, "The hour cometh, and now is, when the true worshippers shall worship the Father in spirit and in truth." The word 'worshipper' in the Greek is *proskunētēs*. One inscription dating to the third century A.D. comes from Syria, and it talks about a decree drawn up for the benefit of "the worshippers who come up". Although the inscription itself was carved in the third century A.D., it incorporates older references going back to the time of the Roman Emperor

Augustus. This supposedly 'Biblical' word occurred outside the Bible after all.

That Samaritan woman was surprised that Jesus showed such prophetic insight concerning her own life. "We know that when the Messiah comes He will tell us all things," she said. Then Jesus told her, "I that speak unto thee am He." Jesus revealed Himself as the Messiah, the Anointed one of God.

"I Am" used of False Gods

One way in which Christ's Deity is shown is by the term *egō eimi*—"I AM." This is an emphatic use of the personal pronoun "I". The word *eimi* in Greek is quite sufficient to say "I am", this being the first person present active of the verb "to be". But added to this in John's Gospel is the personal pronoun *egō*—"I". Thus we are told that our Lord said, "I, even I, AM"—*egō eimi*.

Once again a concept known in current language is given a new spiritual significance. (This practice can be demonstrated at many other places in the Scriptures, as with some of the Psalms of David.)

The expression *egō eimi* was known as 'sacred' language when John wrote his Gospel. Here is one famous inscription about the Egyptian goddess Isis:

> "*I am* Isis, the queen of every land, taught by Hermes, and whatsoever things I have ordained, no one is able to loose them. *I am* the eldest daughter of Cronos, the youngest god. *I am* wife and sister of King Osiris. *I am* the first that devised fruit for men. *I am* mother of Horus the King. *I am* she that riseth in the dog-star."

Over and over again in that inscription Isis is made to use this sacred expression *egō eimi*. The inscription shows how Satan takes the things of God and gives them a false meaning. There is only one who in truth can take to Himself this title "I AM", for this is the title of God Himself. When Moses asked God, "Whom shall I say sent me?" the answer was that the one who was sending him was "I AM" (Exodus 3:14). He is the ever-living, self-existent one.

Many believe that this same teaching is reflected in the term used by the Lord Jesus Christ when He compared Himself with Abraham. "Before Abraham was, I Am", He told the Jews (John 8:58). Abraham 'was'—he appeared for a brief moment on the scene of Bible history and then moved on. Thus Abraham 'was', but Jesus Christ could say "I AM"—the one who always is, for He could say, "Before Abraham was, I AM." He is the true "I AM," the ever-living Son of God.

When the officers came to arrest Jesus He asked them, "Whom do ye seek?" (John 18:4). They said, "Jesus of Nazareth", and He merely said, *"Egō eimi"* —"I Am". At this they fell to the ground, and the Lord repeated His question. To their answer He replied, "I have told you that I Am . . ." As we watch them fall down we realise that puny men could not so much as touch the Son of God until He allowed it. "If therefore ye seek Me, let these go their way," He commanded. How strange—the Prisoner was allowing Himself to be taken, but demanding that His disciples go unharmed! Strange, and yet true.

The way in which this title of God is appropriated by evil powers is also illustrated by one of the so-called magical papyri, dating to the fourth century A.D. It even includes our Lord's teaching, "I am the truth" (John 14:6):

> "*I am* the headless daemon, having eyes in my feet, the strong one, the deathless fire. *I am the truth* who hateth that evil deeds are in the world."

The inscription goes on in blasphemous ways to attribute the powers of God to this power of evil.

The divine usage, *egō eimi*, is there no less than seven times in this one brief passage.

Our Lord Himself said false messiahs would arise, and Paul the Apostle warned that Satan would be as an angel of light. There were indeed false messiahs, but only one true Messiah. False gods were sometimes given this divine title *egō eimi*, but there was only one who could in truth say, "Before Abraham was, I AM". Only He could say "I Am the Good Shepherd", the one who gives His life for the sheep. No evil power claiming deity for himself ever deliberately went to a place of sacrifice because of love for the wandering sheep. As our Lord said, "I am the door of the sheep. All that ever came before Me were *thieves* and robbers (John 10:7, 8).

Only One True Lord

Not only was the title "I AM" attributed to false gods and goddesses, but in many other inscriptions from New Testament times the title 'lord' is given to gods and men. Thus the Egyptian god Serapis is referred to as 'lord', and Roman emperors such as Caligula, Claudius and Nero all took to themselves this same title *kyrios*—'lord'.

A team of Italian archaeologists have recently un-covered a temple devoted to the cult of the so-called "divine emperors". One finely sculptured marble statue was dedicated to "the divine Vespasian".[1] We know that the denarius of Tiberius ascribed divinity to Augustus, and such coins could not be offered in the Jewish treasury because the Jew could acknowledge the Deity of only the true God Jehovah. Our Lord's masterly answer to the Jews' question about paying tribute to Caesar—"Render unto Caesar the things that are Caesar's and to God the things that are Gods"—is possibly a poiner to His knowledge of the false claim to deity by the Caesars.

In the years that followed the disciples and the Apostles made their protest against others who falsely claimed deity. They knew that the title 'Lord' belonged only to Jesus Christ. Paul the Apostle emphasises that Jesus Christ is the true Lord, and he tells us that "every tongue shall confess that Jesus Christ is Lord, to the glory of God the Father" (Philippians 2:11). Throughout the New Testament writings there is a constant protest against the concept of any other being Lord.

In the years beyond the New Testament men went into martyrdom rather than acknowledge any Caesar as Lord. We read of one Christian martyr named Speratus whose answer to the demand to "swear by our lord the emperor" was, "I know no imperium of this world . . . I know my Lord, the King of Kings, and Emperor of all nations".[2]

Some scholars go so far as to suggest that the distinctive title "The Lord's Day" was itself a protest—a stand against the emperors who falsely took to themselves deity. Emperors were 'given' certain days, in honour of themselves. In particular, a monthly day became known in the Roman world as "the Emperor's day".

The Christian recognised the first day of the week as "the Lord's Day", the day on which Christ showed Himself King of Kings and Lord of Lords by rising from the dead. No emperor of Rome, nor any devilish power, could hold Him captive, and on the Lord's Day He demonstrated His final authority. Jesus Christ is the King of Kings (Revelation 17:14). He is Lord of Lords—this is the Name inscribed on His clothing in the picture given of Him ruling the nations with a rod of iron (Revelation 19:15, 16).

"The Scripture cannot Be Broken"
John's Gospel does not only insist on the Deity of the Lord Jesus Christ. It also stands firmly on the divine inspiration of all the Old Testament Scriptures. We find

that the Old Testament is referred to as "the Scripture", as at John 10:35 where we read that "the Scripture"—*graphē* in Greek—"cannot be broken". This usage beautifully illustrates the meaning of this word *graphē* or 'writing'. In New Testament times the term was common in legal phraseology, and it referred to a royal decree which could not be changed.

In our concluding chapter we shall consider some of the background to the trial and crucifixion of Jesus Christ, but as we conclude this section it is relevant to say that the papyrus has endorsed Scripture's own claims as to its validity.

REFERENCES

[1] *Buried History* 4 (June 1968), p. 56.
[2] Deissmann, A. *Light From The Ancient East*, p. 360.

13

The Trial And Crucifixion
Of Jesus Christ

The central theme of the Gospels, and indeed of all
the Scripture, is the redemption offered to the world
by the Lord Jesus Christ. The story of His trial and
crucifixion is recorded in each of the Gospels, and in
this brief survey we look at some points on which
archaeology has bearing. There are also literary records
which are relevant, such as the writings of the Roman
senator and historian Tacitus, who wrote in the late
first and early second centuries A.D. He mentioned that
Christ was put to death by Pontius Pilate in the reign
of Tiberius,[1] just as the New Testament claims (e.g.
at Luke 23:24).

*The Comment by Josephus ... and other Historical
Documents*
One famous comment about Christ is that by
Josephus,[2] saying that the tribe of Christians was so
named from Christ, who appeared alive the third
day after He had been condemned to the cross.
Opinions vary as to whether this is an authentic writ-
ing or whether it is a re-casting by Christians of what
Josephus actually said.

However, by normally accepted academic standards,
the evidence is overwhelming as to the historical Christ.
This can be demonstrated by a comparison of the New

Testament documents with secular records. Instead of great gaps between the records and their first copies, there is a continuous flow of copies of New Testament documents from the century in which they were first written, right down to modern times. But compare this with secular writings: between the Roman writer Horace and the first copies of his works there is a nine-hundred-year gap, and even between the writings of Julius Caesar and the first copies there is again a nine-hundred-year break. Similarly with Livy there is a five hundred-year interval, and with the Roman writer Virgil a gap of about 350 years.

The story is very different with the New Testament documents. We shall see that a fragment of John's Gospel has been found in Egypt, which was circulating within a generation of the death of the Gospel writer himself. In the days of church writers such as Polycarp (who lived from A.D. 69 to A.D. 155) there are many references to the Gospels. Polycarp also quotes the Acts of the Apostles and various Epistles. For instance, in one of his letters (to the Philippians) he speaks of "Jesus Christ who endured to come so far as death for our sins, Whom God raised having loosed the pains of death"—there he quotes Acts 2:24.

Pilate a Historic Figure

Perhaps at this point it is relevant to mention that we do not accept the so-called account of "The Crucifixion of Christ, by an Eye-Witness", which was foisted on to the world at the beginning of this century. It appears to have been based on a romantic fictional reconstruction by K. H. Venturini, dating a hundred years before. Nor do we accept the so-called "Report of Pilate", nor "The Confession of Pontius Pilate". These have long ago been exposed as hoaxes.[3] This is not to say that Pilate is not attested as a historical figure—he is well-known in Jewish history.

Pilate is known historically as the Roman governor of Judaea ('Prefect' was his Roman title at this time). From ancient literature we know that he was a cruel man, selfishly ambitious and hated by the Jews, many of whom he had ruthlessly slaughtered. Although Pilate has been well-known in literature, it was only in 1961 that the first actual historical monument mentioning him came to light. This was an inscription found in the arena at Caesarea referring to Pilate, the Prefect of Judaea.

At John 19:13, towards the end of the account of our Lord's trial, there is reference to the Pavement, *Gabbatha* as it is in Hebrew. Soldiers played games of dice there while prisoners were being tried. An area identified as the Pavement has recently been excavated, and inscribed in the stones was a circle in which was a pattern where such a game could be played. It is challenging to consider that probably in this area the soldiers ridiculed Christ, even putting a crown of thorns on His head as they paid mock allegiance to Him. "They that would destroy me, being mine enemies wrongfully, are mighty," we read at Psalm 69:4. In yet another prophecy about the Messiah we read at Psalm 22, "I am a reproach of men, and despised of the people . . . All they that see me laugh me to scorn . . . The assembly of the wicked have enclosed me." Little did those same soldiers realise that they were about to fulfil another prophecy in that same Psalm at verse 18, "They part my garments among them, and cast lots upon my vesture".

Another prophecy relating to the Messiah was Zechariah 11:12, 13—He would be sold for thirty pieces of silver. This was the price of a slave, and recent research has shown that originally it was an idiomatic expression indicating contempt for that which was virtually worthless.[4]

The Earliest New Testament Writing

The name of Pontius Pilate is familiar in connection with the trial of Christ. Pilate declared that Jesus was innocent, but delivered Him to death by crucifixion. The earliest fragment of a copy of the New Testament writings is a part of John's Gospel relating to the trial of Christ before Pilate.

One side of this fragment has part of John 18:31–33, translated in the Authorised Version as follows:

> "Then said Pilate unto them, Take ye Him and judge Him according to your law. The Jews therefore said unto him, It is not lawful for us to put any man to death, that the saying of Jesus might be fulfilled which He spake, signifying what death He should die. Then Pilate entered into the judgment hall again and called Jesus and said unto Him, Art Thou the King of the Jews?"

The other side of the fragment has part of John 18:37, 38, and again in the Authorised Version this reads:

> "Pilate therefore said unto Him, Art Thou a King then? Jesus answered, Thou sayest that I am a King. To this end was I born and for this cause came I into the world, that I should bear witness unto the truth. Every one that is of the truth heareth My voice. Pilate said unto Him, What is truth? And when he had said this he went out again unto the Jews and said unto them, I find in Him no fault at all."

It seems significant that this is the earliest copy of any portion of the New Testament discovered. It dates to within twenty-five years of the death of John, the aged Apostle who wrote this portion of Scripture. Within one generation of his death John's Gospel was already circulating in Egypt, hundreds of miles from where he wrote the original.

Jesus said, "My words shall not pass away." No other ancient book can compare with the Bible writings, which have been so uniquely preserved through the centuries. Nor has any other ancient book been verified in the remarkable ways which have been true of the Bible, God's Word of Truth.

Pilate wanted to release Jesus, but to avoid his own responsibility he sent Him to Herod who was in Jerusalem at that time. Herod ridiculed Jesus, urging Him to perform a miracle, but even Herod had to send Jesus back to Pilate with a declaration as to His innocence.

At many points we find that the trial of Jesus Christ is accurately recorded, and bears the hallmark of eye-witness reporting. Thus we find examples of Roman procurators prepared to release a prisoner in adherence to the demands of the multitude.[5] We even read of a prefect who scourged the prisoner and then delivered him over to a local official at the demand of the people. This can be put alongside John 19:1 where we read that Pilate scourged Jesus, and Mark 15:15 where we learn that Pilate, "willing to content the people, released Barabbas unto them, and delivered Jesus, when he had scourged Him, to be crucified."

They Dripped—With Blood

Pilate had wanted to release Jesus, but was frightened to do so because the crowd said that if he let Jesus go, who announced Himself as King of the Jews, Pilate himself was not Caesar's friend. Pilate feared that such a charge could lead to his own dismissal, or even worse! Pilate would not take that risk, and so he called for water to signify that he was not guilty of the blood of this just Man.

Pilate took that bowl of water and washed his hands saying, "I am innocent of the blood of this just Person: see YE to it." But Pilate could not wash away his guilt with water. And in modern times he has been pictured as one who through the days, the months, the years, the centuries, was constantly rinsing his immaculate hands in clear, cold water—and then forever holding them up to examine them, only to shrink in horror. For they dripped—with blood.

The chief priests were also guilty, for it was their choice to reject Jesus Christ. Ancient papyrus letters from Egypt add colour to the words of the crowd who cried, "Away with Him! We will not have this Man to reign over us." One letter was from a boy who was annoyed because his father had not taken him on a holiday to Alexandria. He was very *'upset'* at this, and used the same word as is used in the Acts of the Apostles at chapter 17:6 where the Apostles were accused of having "*turned* the world *upside down*". This boy quoted his mother as he wrote, "And my mother said to Archaelaus, 'He upsets me—away with him!'" Here our schoolboy used yet another New Testament phrase as he repeated the words, "Away with him!" This expression was used by the Jewish crowd when they cried concerning our Lord, "Away with Him!" (John 19:15).

We read at John 19:16, 17 that Jesus was led away, and He went to Golgotha—the Place of a Skull— to be crucified. The place is called Calvary at Luke 23:33, this coming from the Latin word meaning 'skull'. *Golgotha* is Hebrew or Aramaic for 'skull', so clearly the words have a similar meaning. There the Lord Jesus Christ was crucified.

Again we find an interesting word in a papyrus document that tells of a Roman senator who is visiting Egypt to see the sights.[6] This word for 'sights', *theōrian*, is also used of the crucifixion of Christ. We read that all the people came together to that *sight* (Luke 23:48), where the Lord of life and glory was about to die, and He became a Spectacle to be gazed at. How amazing is the grace of God—His Son was to be regarded as a 'sight' which people came to behold, even as the Roman senator in this papyrus was to behold the sights of ancient Egypt.

Another word used in this document is *psōmion*. The official was to be provided with a '*bun*' to feed to the crocodiles, and this is a form of the same word used at John 13:26ff. where we read of our Lord giving the favoured portion, "the sop", to Judas Iscariot.

The Inscription in Three Languages

At John 19:20 we read that the inscription over the cross was written in three languages—Hebrew, Latin and Greek. One interesting aspect of the findings of the Dead Sea Scrolls was the realisation that Hebrew was more widely used in New Testament times than had previously been thought. Letters were written in Hebrew, indicating that this was not simply a dead priestly language. While it is true that by New Testament times the word 'Hebrew' actually embraced the sister language Aramaic as well, it is worth noting that the Gospel writer might well have meant Hebrew and not Aramaic when he referred to the inscription over the cross.

Another significant conclusion from the Dead Sea Scrolls is that the background to John's Gospel is Judean, and not Hellenistic. John uses contrasting concepts such as "light and darkness" and various other expressions which were Jewish in background, as shown by their use at Qumran. "Sons of light", "brotherly love", "fountain of living water", "truth and perversity"—these are common to John and Qumran.

Reading a Scroll at Nazareth

The argument as to our Lord's knowledge of Hebrew applies also to that delightful incident where He read from the Scroll of Isaiah—it was Hebrew that He read, the portion being part of Isaiah 61—"The Spirit of the

Lord God is upon Me; because the Lord hath anointed Me to preach good tidings unto the meek; He hath sent Me to bind up the brokenhearted, to proclaim liberty to the captives, and the opening of the prison to them that are bound."

Our Lord read this aloud in that synagogue at Nazareth, the town where He had been brought up. The incident is recorded at Luke 4:16–30. Our Lord included the first clause of Isaiah 61:2—"to proclaim the acceptable year of the Lord"—but He did not go on to the next clause which tells of the day of God's vengeance. That latter time had not yet arrived, but our Lord Himself stated concerning the first parts of the passage, "This day is this Scripture fulfilled in your ears" (verse 21). He Himself was the one who was chosen to preach good tidings, to bind up the brokenhearted, to proclaim liberty to captives: for He Himself was God manifest in flesh, and our Redeemer. How tragic to realise that though this Scripture was fulfilled for the Jews that day in their own ears, yet this one, the greatest Prophet of all time, was without honour in His own country. This He Himself declared in this context (verse 24).

We can sense the hush as our Lord rolled up the Scroll and handed it back to the attendant, according to custom. He then expounded the passage, as also was the practice. What a privilege for those people in the synagogue at Nazareth! It is little wonder we read, "The eyes of them that were in the synagogue were fastened on Him" (verse 20); and, "All bare Him witness, and wondered at the gracious words which proceeded out of His mouth" (verse 22).

And as we continue to listen to His words as they are recorded in the Gospels, we too wonder at the gracious words that came from His lips.

REFERENCES

[1] Tacitus. *The Annals Of Imperial Rome*. Translated by Michael Grant, p. 354.

[2] Whiston, W. (translator). *The Life And Works Of Flavius Josephus*, p. 535.

[3] Discussed at length in: Goodspeed, E. J. *Famous 'Biblical' Hoaxes*, 1956.

[4] *Buried History* 5 (March 1969), pp. 5, 6.

[5] Deissmann, A. *Light From The Ancient East*, pp. 266–267, Florentine Pap. No. 61.

[6] Milligan, G. *Selections From The Greek Papyri*, p. 30, Tebtunis Pap. No. 33, 12 B.C.

Conclusion

From some of these documents from tne 'talking crocodiles' and elsewhere we have selected examples to illustrate various aspects of the New Testament writings. It would be so easy to over-emphasise the significance of these documents. And yet their importance is great, not only in making known to us words previously unknown, not only bringing to life New Testament scenes by showing us similar sketches dating to approximately the same times, but also by leading us firmly and reverently back to a deepened appreciation of the uniqueness of the Canonical Gospels and the rest of the New Testament.

Bibliography

The books and journals consulted in the preparation of this volume include the following:

BOOKS

Allen, I. *The Early Church And The New Testament* (London, New York, Toronto: Longmans, Green & Co., 1951).

Baikie, J. *Egyptian Papyri And Papyrus-Hunting* (London: The Religious Tract Society, 1925).

Beasley, W. J. *The Amazing Story Of Sodom* (Melbourne: The Australian Institute of Archaeology, 1957. Gospel Literature Service, Bombay).

Bell, H. Idris. *Jews And Christians In Egypt* (London: The British Museum, 1924. Oxford University Press).

Bell, H. Idris, and Skeat, T. C. *Fragments Of An Unknown Gospel And Other Early Christian Papyri* (London: Trustees of the British Museum, 1935. University Press, Oxford).

Benson, C. H. *A Guide For Bible Study*.

Bettenson, H. (Editor). *Documents Of The Christian Church* (London, New York, Toronto: Oxford University Press, 1954).

Bishop, E. F. F. *Jesus Of Palestine. The Local Background To The Gospel Documents* (London: Lutterworth Press, 1955).

Bruce, F. F. *Second Thoughts On The Dead Sea Scrolls* (London: The Paternoster Press, 1961).

David, M., and van Groningen, B. A. *Papyrological Primer* (Leyden: E. J. Brill, 1952).

Deissmann, A. *Light From The Ancient East. The New Testa-*

ment Illustrated By Recently Discovered Texts Of The Graeco-Roman World. Translated by Lionel R.M.Strachan. (London: Hodder & Stoughton, 1st edition, 1910).

Farrar, F. W. *The Messages Of The Books* (London: Macmillan & Co., 1884).

Furness, J. M. *Vital Words Of The Bible* (Michigan: Wm. B. Eerdmans Publishing Co., 1966).

Goodspeed, E. J. *Famous 'Biblical' Hoaxes* (Michigan: Baker Book House, 1956).

Grenfell, B. P., and Hunt, A. S. (Translators and Editors). *The Oxyrhynchus Papyri*. Part II (London: Egypt Exploration Fund, Graeco-Roman Branch, 1899. University Press, Oxford).

—— Part IV (London: Egypt Exploration Fund, Graeco-Roman Branch, 1904. University Press, Oxford).

—— (Translators and Editors). *Sayings Of Our Lord From An Early Greek Papyrus* (London: Henry Frowde, 1897, for the Egypt Exploration Fund).

Head, E. D. *New Testament Life And Literature As Reflected In The Papyri* (Nashville, Tennessee: Broadman Press, 1952).

Henry, C. F. H. (Editor). *Jesus Of Nazareth: Saviour And Lord* (London: The Tyndale Press, 1966).

Hunt, A. S., and Smyly, J. G. (Editors). *The Tebtunis Papyri*. Volume III, Part I. (London: Egypt Exploration Society, Graeco-Roman Memoirs, 1933. Humphrey Milford, Oxford University Press).

James, M. R. *The Apocryphal New Testament* (Oxford: The Clarendon Press, 1950).

Milligan, G. *Selections From The Greek Papyri* (Cambridge: University Press, 1912).

Moulton, J. H. *From Egyptian Rubbish Heaps* (London: Charles H. Kelly, 1916).

Moulton, J. H., and Milligan, G. *The Vocabulary Of The Greek Testament Illustrated From The Papyri And Other Non-Literary Sources* (London: Hodder & Stoughton, 1957).

Ramsay, Sir William. *The Bearing Of Recent Discoveries On The Trustworthiness Of The New Testament* (London, New York, Toronto: Hodder & Stoughton, 2nd edition, 1915).
—— *St. Paul The Traveller And The Roman Citizen* (London: Hodder & Stoughton, 1925).

Smith, D. *Unwritten Sayings Of Our Lord* (London, New York, Toronto: Hodder & Stoughton, 1913).

Tacitus. *The Annals Of Imperial Rome.* Translated by Michael Grant (The Penguin Classics, 1961).
Tenney, M. C. *New Testament Times* (Michigan: Wm. B Eerdmans Book Co., 1965).
Thompson, J. A. *The Bible And Archaeology* (Excter, Devon, England: The Paternoster Press, 1962).

Turner, N. *Grammatical Insights Into The New Testament* (Edinburgh: T. & T. Clark, 1965).

Unger, M. F. *Archaeology And The New Testament* (Michigan: Zondervan Publishing House, 1962).
van Unnik, W. C. *Newly Discovered Gnostic Writings* (London: S.C.M. Press, 1960).

Whiston, W. (Translator). *The Life And Works Of Flavius Josephus* (Philadelphia: The John C. Winston Co., standard edition).

Wilson, R. McL. *The Gospel Of Philip* (London: A. R. Mowbray & Co. Ltd., 1962).

The Gospel According To Thomas (duplicated copy in the library of the Australian Institute of Archaeology).

JOURNALS

Biblical Archaeologist (published by the American Schools of Oriental Research).
Bulletin Of The American Schools Of Oriental Research.
Bulletin Of The John Rylands Library, Manchester.
Buried History (Melbourne: The Australian Institute of Archaeology).

Christianity Today (Washington, D.C.: Wilbur D. Benedict).
Journal Of Egyptian Archaeology (London: Egypt Exploration Fund).
Palestine Exploration Quarterly (London: Palestine Exploration Fund and British School of Archaeology in Jerusalem).

ABBREVIATIONS

J.E.A.   Journal Of Egyptian Archaeology.
Oxy. Pap. Oxyrhynchus Papyrus.

Index of Persons, Places And Subjects

Virgil 109

Wellhausen, J. 80

Index of Biblical References